*Prince Henry the Navigator*

# THE WORLD'S GREAT EXPLORERS

## *Henry the Navigator*

By Charnan Simon

Consultant: James A. Casada, Ph.D.,
Professor of History,
Winthrop University,
Rock Hill, South Carolina

**CHILDRENS PRESS®**

CHICAGO

*Portuguese memorial coin com-*
*memorating Henry the Navigator*

*For T.K., a prince among men*

Project Editor: Ann Heinrichs
Designer: Lindaanne Donohoe
Cover Art: Steven Gaston Dobson
Engraver: Liberty Photoengraving

**Library of Congress**
**Cataloging-in-Publication Data**

Simon, Charnan.
    Henry the Navigator / by Charnan Simon.
        p.   cm. — (The World's great explorers)
    Includes bibliographical references and index.
    Summary: A biography of the Portuguese
prince whose navigational ideas and innovations had
a significant impact on later explorers.
    ISBN 0-516-03071-X
    1. Henry, Infante of Portugal, 1394-1460—
Juvenile literature. 2. Explorers—Portugal—
Biography—Juvenile literature. [1. Henry, Infante
of Portugal, 1394-1460. 2. Explorers.] I. Title. II.
Series.

G286.H5S56  1993                 92-37048
946.9'02—dc20                    CIP
                                  AC

471216

*Monument to Discoveries in Lisbon, Portugal, with Henry the Navigator at the forward tip*

# Table of Contents

# Chapter 1
# Crusade to Ceuta

**P**rince Henry of Portugal stared intently out to sea. Behind him, across the blue Atlantic, lay his Portuguese homeland. Ahead of him loomed the fabled Strait of Gibraltar, gateway to the Mediterranean Sea. All around him, becalmed in the misty sea, were the more than two hundred ships of the Portuguese fleet.

Prince Henry turned impatiently from his watch. It had been two weeks since the fleet set sail from Lisbon on July 25, 1415. Fog had held them up for a week off the coast of Spain. Then a fire broke out aboard one ship, and the deadly plague on another. Now here was fog again to delay their passage through the narrow Strait of Gibraltar. How much longer would it be before they could fulfill their mission?

And what a mission it was, too. In his mind's eye, Prince Henry stared through the sea mist, past the fabled strait, all the way to the North African port city of Ceuta—his destination and his destiny.

For three years, Henry—along with his father, King John, and his brothers Duarte and Pedro—had planned this expedition to conquer Ceuta. The city was a great trading center for the Moors, the Muslim people of North Africa. It was perfectly positioned to control sea trade in the Mediterranean. It was also the last stop on the caravan route that brought gold and slaves from central Africa. With Ceuta under its command, reasoned King John and his sons, Portugal would control some of the richest trading in the world. The Christian country of Portugal would control it—not their sworn Muslim enemies.

For hundreds of years, Christians and Muslims had clashed bitterly in Europe and the Middle East. Each believed the other to be their mortal enemy. Christianity was based on the teachings of Jesus Christ, whom Christians believed to be the Savior, the Messiah, the Son of God.

The Muslim religion of Islam, which was founded some six hundred years after Jesus lived, was based on the teachings of the prophet Muhammad. Muslims saw Muhammad as the Seal of the Prophets. It was Muhammad who had built on and perfected the earlier teachings of such other great prophets as Abraham, Moses, and Jesus.

For Christians, the Islamic belief that Jesus was just another prophet was heresy. For Muslims, the Christian refusal to acknowledge Muhammad's greatness was equally blasphemous. It was an unresolvable argument that would lead to countless wars and cruel acts of bloodshed over hundreds of years.

In this expedition of 1415, King John and his followers saw Portugal's chance to strike a blow against the hated Muslim Moors on their own North African

*The Kasbah Mosque in Morocco*

soil. Taking Ceuta was a holy crusade—and twenty-one-year-old Prince Henry couldn't wait for it to begin.

Finally, the fog lifted enough for the Portuguese captains to cautiously pilot their ships through the treacherous strait. But before they could position themselves for battle, a great gale blew up. The fleet was scattered throughout the Mediterranean Sea. By now, King John had had just about enough. Perhaps the expedition was jinxed. Perhaps his councillors were right, and it would be better to turn back to Portugal while they still could.

If King John had doubts, his sons didn't share them. Henry, Duarte, and Pedro rose up with one voice to insist that the crusade must go on as planned. You didn't turn your back on a holy mission just because of a little bad weather!

Bolstered by his sons' enthusiasm, King John gave the command. At daybreak on August 21, the royal fleet of Portugal would attack the Moorish citadel at Ceuta. They would not retreat until Ceuta was taken.

All through the night of August 20, the Portuguese fleet prepared itself. Ships were regrouped and anchored in position for storming the shores at daybreak. Noblemen fitted their armor; archers strung their bows; foot soldiers sharpened their swords and tested the weight of their battle-axes. Prince Henry readied himself, too. His father had promised him the honor of being the first man to land on the beach.

Across the bay at Ceuta, preparations were also taking place. Sala-ben-Sala, the governor of Ceuta, was worried. Earlier that week, when he had first spied the Portuguese, he had ordered up extra soldiers from the hills behind his city. Then, when the gale scattered the fleet, he had sent those soldiers home again. Now that the fleet was back in position, Sala-ben-Sala was in a bind. There wasn't time to call up additional soldiers. In a desperate show of defiance, he had every window and doorway in Ceuta lit with candles. This would show those Portuguese how well populated and prepared Ceuta was.

Scornfully, the Portuguese responded by lighting up every one of their more than two hundred ships. *They* weren't frightened by Sala-ben-Sala's bluff.

Such was the situation as the sun rose on the warm summer morning of August 21. To Henry's frustration, he wasn't the first Christian to set foot on this infidel territory. Another nobleman, overcome by impatience, jumped off the ship ahead of him. Not to be outdone, Henry called his trumpeters to sound the charge. Leaping into a small boat, he went ashore.

The fighting was swift and savage. Henry and his followers stormed the beach, fought their way through the main gate, and poured into the city. Triumphant, Henry planted his banner on a hill (which turned out to be the city's main garbage heap)—the first Christian flag to fly over North African territory.

*King John I of Portugal*

The fighting grew more desperate as the Moors realized they were outnumbered. Swords clashed in the narrow alleys, arrows whistled, and the groans of the wounded filled the air.

At one point, Henry's followers lost sight of him in the confusion. Word was sent to King John, encamped near the city's gates, that his son was dead. Stoically, King John replied, "Such is the end that soldiers must expect."

But Henry wasn't dead. Fighting with the strength and courage of ten men, he had hacked his way to the very door of the citadel itself. Surrounded by his enemies, he managed to hold off all comers until Portuguese reinforcements finally arrived.

By late afternoon the battle was over. Those Moors who had not been killed had fled into the hills behind the city. The Muslim mosque was consecrated as a Christian church, and King John called for the first service to be held on Sunday morning. There, before the nobles of his kingdom, King John knighted his three sons, Duarte, Pedro, and Henry, in God's holy service. The conquest of Ceuta was complete.

Yet, for Prince Henry, Ceuta was only the beginning. This conquest would prove to be more than just a victory for his country and his faith, more than just a chance for a young prince to earn his knighthood. In taking Ceuta, Prince Henry put in motion events that would change the world forever.

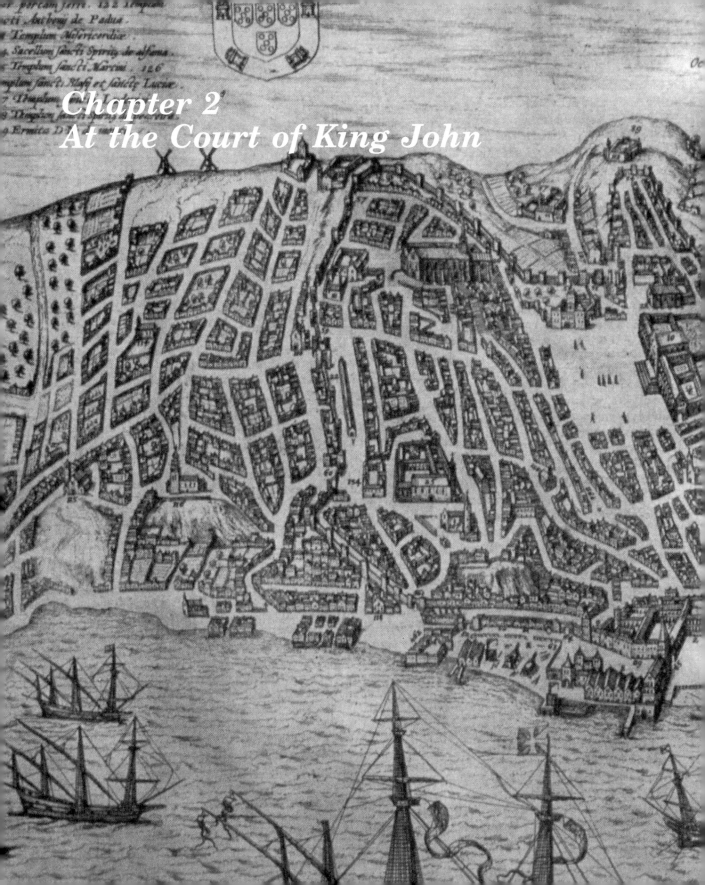

# Chapter 2
# At the Court of King John

The Portugal of Prince Henry's boyhood was a young kingdom and a small one. Henry's father, King John, had had to fight for control of his country against both warring Portuguese nobles and invading armies of nearby Spanish Castile. Much of his youth had been spent in battle. It wasn't until 1385 that he finally subdued the Castilians and united his own nobles under one flag and one kingdom.

King John worked hard to make his kingdom successful. The common people had always liked him, and now he strove to earn the support and respect of his nobles. He rewrote Portugal's criminal laws, encouraged the use of Portuguese instead of Latin in everyday business, and made the royal court at Lisbon an honorable place to live and work. In foreign affairs, King John carefully nurtured the uneasy peace with Castile. He encouraged trade with neighboring lands such as England, Burgundy, and Flanders.

*Princess Isabel*

*Philip of Burgundy*

In all that he did, King John had a strong helpmate in his wife, Queen Philippa. The sister of England's King Henry IV, Philippa was a favorite with the Portuguese people. Devoutly Christian, she brought discipline and refinement to what had once been a rather rowdy royal family.

King John and Queen Philippa took as much care of their family as they did of their country. Their six children—Duarte, Pedro, Henry, Isabel, John, and Fernando—were educated by the best standards of the day. The five boys read Latin, Greek, and Portuguese, as well as French, the language of their mother's English court at that time. They argued philosophy and science, read tales of knightly chivalry, and became expert horsemen and huntsmen. And, always, they were each other's best friends. As Duarte put it, "We put up with each other's peculiarities . . . and never was there any jealousy among us."

Isabel, being a girl, was educated differently. Queen Philippa raised her daughter to be a pious, idealistic Christian, just as she herself was. In due time, Isabel would do what most princesses did—she would leave home and enter into a politically wise marriage within another noble family. In Isabel's case, marrying Duke Philip of Burgundy cemented relations between Portugal and the rich Burgundian court.

By the year 1411, the future was looking bright for Portugal. A lasting treaty had finally been signed with Castile, promising peace for the next one hundred and one years. Portugal was prosperous, the princes and princess were growing up happy and healthy—it was time to celebrate!

In true medieval style, King John chose to celebrate with a jousting tournament. His three eldest

*The marriage of Isabel of Portugal to Philip of Burgundy*

sons were old enough to be knighted—Duarte was 20, Pedro was 19, and Henry was 17—and King John meant to do it up right. Knights from all over Europe would be invited, the jousts would go on for a year, the prizes would be extravagant beyond compare. As King John announced, "I shall give presents of such magnificence . . . that the greatness and pleasantness of these gifts will oblige these lords to speak of them with admiration to all their friends."

If King John expected his sons to be pleased by his plans, he was sorely disappointed. "Let us think about it," they said diplomatically. Among themselves, they were more blunt. Staged tournaments might be all right for merchants' sons. But they were princes! Had not their father, King John, earned his knighthood in real battle? Surely they deserved no less. Raised in the lore of the chivalrous Christian knight, Henry and his brothers had no desire to win their knighthood through some silly game.

Thus was born the idea of the attack on Ceuta. The young princes knew all about the holy wars between Christians and Muslims. They knew how, between the years 711 and 1249, the Moors of North Africa had invaded and ruled most of the Iberian Peninsula (Portugal and Spain). They also knew how, beginning in 1064, Christian soldiers from all over Europe had fought to drive their Muslim enemies out of the Iberian Peninsula—and then out of the Holy Lands of the Middle East. These battles, known as the Crusades, had taken thousands of lives. In the end, Portugal and most of Spain were taken back by Christian armies, but Jerusalem was still in Muslim hands.

Prince Henry and his brothers knew their tiny country was not strong enough to win back Jerusalem. But Ceuta was a different matter. It, too, was a Muslim stronghold. From it, the Moors might someday try to invade the Iberian Peninsula again. Furthermore, Muslim ships from Ceuta often attacked Christian trading vessels in the Mediterranean. Driving out the Moors and setting up a Portuguese fortress in Ceuta would be the first check to Muslim power on their own continent. All of Europe would breathe easier knowing that Christians held Ceuta.

There were other reasons for attacking Ceuta. It was a bustling Mediterranean trade center and controlled sea traffic through the Strait of Gibraltar. All goods from Africa and Asia bound for the Atlantic passed through Ceuta.

Portugal and the other European states depended on these goods. They were necessities, not luxuries. Without African gold, royal treasuries would be empty. Without Indonesian pepper, cinnamon, ginger, and nutmeg, European foodstuffs would rot. And without Chinese opiates and herbs, healers would have almost no medicines with which to treat their patients.

Of course, there were luxury items as well. Silks from China and damask from Asia Minor were the preferred fabrics of Europe's nobility. Fragrant Arabian ambergris, musk, and attar of roses were used to perfume a population that bathed only infrequently. And everyone knew the value of Ceylonese pearls and Indian diamonds.

The problem was, Muslims controlled the trade routes along which these goods traveled. With the Moors in command of Ceuta and other Mediterranean ports, Christian Europe could buy only what Muslims wanted to sell. Even then, Europeans had to pay exorbitant prices to the Italian sailors the Moors used as middlemen. How much more profitable it would be if Portugal held Ceuta instead of the Moors!

This was the reasoning Prince Henry and his brothers used to convince King John to stage a real military attack instead of a mock tournament. King John listened to all the arguments. Then he sent for Prince Henry separately. "For it seemed to me," he said, "that you had more to say about this than your brothers. Tell me what you really think!"

*Prince Henry*

It was the chance Henry had been waiting for. Of all the princes, none wanted the expedition to Ceuta so much as he. Eloquently and persuasively, Henry presented his case. When he was finished, King John embraced him, saying, "There is no need for further argument. With the help of God I will begin this enterprise and continue it to the end. And since you and I have been together in making this decision, you must be the one to carry the news to your brothers."

It was a great honor for a seventeen-year-old prince. Even greater was the next honor King John conferred. Henry was to assemble most of the Portuguese fleet from the northern city of Oporto. Prince Pedro would gather some of the fleet at Lisbon, under the watchful eye of his father. But Henry would be acting on his own authority. This was resounding proof of the confidence his father had in him. And so the preparations began. Spies were sent to scout out the Ceuta harbor. False messages were passed around Europe to mislead the rest of the world as to Portugal's real purpose. Ships were hired from abroad, while Pedro and Henry collected, built, and manned others from home.

Everyone in Portugal was caught up in the excitement. For three years, it seemed that the Portuguese people worked at nothing else but preparing for war. Overturned ships lined the riversides, with caulkers working day and night to mend their hulls and make them seaworthy. Side by side with the ships lay hundreds of slaughtered oxen and cattle. While some men skinned the carcasses, others cut and salted the meat, while still others packed it in barrels.

Fishermen and their wives were busy up and down the coast, netting, gutting, and salting their fish. Every free bit of ground was covered with gleaming silver scales. In the towns, bakers kept their oven fires burning around the clock, baking hard biscuits for the salted meats and fish. Wine makers increased their grape harvests, and olive growers pressed more oil.

Throughout the country, one could hear the steady hammering of carpenters and coopers, making and repairing the boxes and barrels that would be needed to carry all the supplies. Tailors were kept busy sewing undergarments and uniforms, while metal workers fashioned the armor plate that would protect noble Portuguese knights in the field. The knights themselves, along with their squires, cleaned and polished and sharpened their swords and battle-axes. Gunsmiths fitted up new artillery, and rope makers laid mile after mile of strong, unbreakable cord.

By early summer of 1415, the expedition was ready. But even as Prince Henry triumphantly brought his fleet into the Lisbon harbor, tragedy struck. Queen Philippa, his beloved mother, was ill with the dreaded plague. Since 1347 the black plague had been the scourge of Europe. In a mere two years, from 1347 to 1349, nearly one-third of western Europe's population had been wiped out by this disease. For the next four hundred years, scarcely a decade would pass without a new outbreak.

Now Queen Philippa had fallen victim. Grief-stricken, Prince Henry and his father and brothers gathered by her bedside. Under no circumstances, this brave woman ordered, was their mission to be delayed by her illness or death. She wished only to present her sons with pieces of the True Cross, and with the swords she had had specially made for them to use in this holy battle.

This accomplished, Queen Philippa fell back on her pillow. Legend has it that she made one last request: "Remain always as you have been, my sons—loving and united. In my country, we have a story about the arrow. Take one arrow by itself, and it is nothing—you can snap it in your hands. But if you hold many of them together, it is beyond your strength to break them." As darkness grew in the room, a strong wind gusted up from the sea.

"What wind is that?" asked the queen.

"It is a wind from the north," they told her.

"A good wind for your journey," she murmured.

Then, as the wind gusted and wailed, and her children gathered around her, the good, brave queen breathed her last. King John and his children were devastated. All of them had relied on this woman,

*Queen Philippa*

whom they felt was the best possible wife and mother. What were they to do now?

It was Prince Henry, as usual, who came up with the answer. Philippa was the staunchest Christian soldier of them all, he argued. She had forbidden them to cancel their crusade because of her. The ships were in the harbor—the supplies were secure in the cargo holds—the soldiers were ready—the expedition to Ceuta must go on as planned.

*Lisbon, seen from the Tagus River*

And so it did. On July 25, 1415, the Portuguese fleet sailed down the Tagus River and into the blue Atlantic. What a sight it was! There were twenty-seven war galleys with three tiers of oars and thirty-two galleys with two tiers. Sixty-three ships were needed to carry the troops and over a hundred to hold the necessary supplies. Some thirty thousand sailors ferried twenty thousand soldiers on their crusade. As one awestruck observer noted, "If all the trees of Portugal had been sawed into planks, and all the men turned carpenters, they never could have made so many ships!"

If the fleet sailed out of Lisbon in triumph, it returned in September crowned with even greater glory. The rout of Ceuta was complete. Duarte, Pedro, and Henry had earned their knighthood, and Portugal had earned the respect and admiration of the entire European community. The year 1415 was indeed fortunate for Prince Henry and his country.

*Lisbon's Belem Tower was the starting point on Portuguese navigators' charts.*

# Chapter 3
# Beyond the Known World

If King John had hoped that Ceuta would make Portugal rich, he was sadly disappointed. As soon as the Moors vanished from the city, so did the vast trade they had once controlled. Ceuta had indeed been the endpoint for caravans coming west from Egypt and Baghdad and north from sub-Saharan Africa. But those caravans were mounted by Muslim traders—traders who were not about to do business with Christians. With the Moors gone, caravan traffic at Ceuta dried up almost overnight.

It was a frustrating experience for King John and his sons. Equally frustrating was the constant military threat to Ceuta from its Muslim neighbors. Things came to a head in 1418, when the Portuguese garrison in Ceuta was threatened by Muslim troops from nearby Granada and Fez.

Hurriedly, King John had Prince Henry take a small relief fleet to Ceuta's aid. By the time Henry arrived, the danger was past. Disappointed that he could not once again prove himself in battle, Henry decided to stay on a few months in the North African port. Ceuta might not need his help. But just 14 miles (23 kilometers) across the strait was the city of Gibraltar. For thousands of years, Gibraltar had been a key Mediterranean port. Now it lay on that part of the Iberian Peninsula that was still under Muslim rule.

To Henry, the Muslim garrison at Gibraltar seemed a perfect target. He sent a message to his father. As long as the fleet was outfitted and ready for a fight, he wanted to attack Gibraltar. Once more, Portuguese forces would drive back the Infidel. With both Gibraltar and Ceuta in its hands, Portugal would command the entire strait. It was a young man's scheme, and it met with solid disapproval from King John. Gibraltar was better fortified and more powerful than Ceuta. Attacking it might aggravate neighboring Spanish Castile, with whom Portugal had only recently made peace. Anyway, with winter coming, the strait would be rough and unpredictable. Under no circumstances was Prince Henry to attempt such a foolhardy venture. He was to return home immediately.

Return Henry did, but not to Lisbon. His brother Duarte was there, busily learning how to rule the kingdom he would one day inherit from his father. Pedro, on the other hand, had set out on a lengthy tour of Europe to see how other courts governed their affairs. But Henry had different ideas. He had spent his time in Ceuta thoughtfully and well. He had spoken with Muslim prisoners and other inhabitants of the town. From them he had learned the routes of camel caravans and had seen maps—some fanciful, some factual—of Africa's interior and of the East. He had learned just how cut off Europe was from the riches of Africa and Asia and just how absolute was Muslim control of all overland routes to those riches.

The more he learned, the more Henry was convinced that Portugal ought to have a share of those riches. But how? King John was having a hard enough time holding on to Ceuta. Fighting the Moors for control of their North African caravan routes was out of

*Duarte of Portugal*

the question. Making peace with Ceuta's Moorish neighbors and striking a deal with the Muslim traders was equally unthinkable.

There was only one thing left to do. If Portugal couldn't conquer the Moors and wouldn't make peace with them, it would just have to bypass them altogether. Since the Moors controlled the overland routes to Africa and Asia, Portugal would control the sea routes. Portugal needn't bother with cumbersome camel caravans. It would send sailing ships right down the African coast and establish its own trading centers with African gold miners. After that, the Portuguese ships would continue sailing down the African coast, around the southern tip, all the way to the Indies.

These were the thoughts filling Henry's mind and firing his imagination as he returned to Portugal in 1418. Shunning Lisbon and other civilized cities, he set up housekeeping on a bleak, windswept cape at the southwesternmost tip of the Iberian Peninsula. Here, at the Sacred Cape of Sagres, with the Atlantic pounding all around him, Prince Henry stared out to sea and plotted his life's course.

There were, he knew, a few obstacles to overcome. First, no one even knew if Africa *had* a southern tip, or if it were, instead, connected to another land mass. Certainly no one in living memory had ever sailed down the African coast—not as far as Henry planned to go. Legend had it that, some two thousand years earlier, a sailor named Hanno, from the North African city of Carthage, had sailed nearly 3,000 miles (4,830 kilometers) south along the west coast of Africa. Around that same time, another intrepid crew sailed from Phoenicia, an ancient land along the Mediterranean coasts of present-day Syria, Lebanon, and Israel. Supposedly, the Phoenicians sailed all the way around Africa from east to west—a journey lasting well over two years. As legends went, these were fine—but legends don't leave maps and navigation guides.

Legends do, however, sometimes leave a residue of fear—which was another of Prince Henry's obstacles. In the fifteenth century, seamen who had never sailed the Atlantic nevertheless knew the ocean by any number of sinister nicknames. The Dark Ocean, the Sea of Obscurity, the Sea of Darkness—these were just a few of the names that sea captains called that great unknown sea. Along with the nicknames came the stories. There were monsters living in the Sea of Darkness, and horrid slime. In the south, the sun burned so hot that the waters boiled. Magnetic rocks pulled the iron fastenings right out of a ship's side. Those seamen who sailed far enough would be swept over the edge of the earth in a huge, shimmering waterfall.

Prince Henry didn't believe any of these stories. To him, an ocean was just an ocean—a highway begging to be traveled. With the right ships, the right maps, the right navigation aids, and the right sailors, you could sail anywhere you chose.

*Hanno, of ancient Carthage, sailing for the west coast of Africa*

On the other hand, Henry knew that no one in his time had ever sailed more than about a thousand miles (1,600 kilometers) down the African coast, to a place called Cape Bojador. He knew that the northwest winds and strong ocean currents made sailing home from any African expedition difficult at best—and fatal at worst. Even if a ship could push its way against the wind and avoid dangerous rocks and currents, it was likely to run into Moorish pirates and so end in tragedy.

Still, Prince Henry was determined to overcome all these obstacles. And now it was more than just the riches of the East that spurred him on. Henry's curiosity had been awakened. The thought of the unknown world, waiting to be made known, constantly gnawed at him. Let Duarte learn how to rule a kingdom. Let Pedro learn how other kingdoms were ruled. He, Henry, would learn what no man before him had ever known. And he would do so for the simple reason that "he had a wish to know the land that lay beyond . . . that Cape called Bojador, for that up to his time, neither by writings, nor by the memory of man, was known with any certainty the nature of the land beyond that Cape."

King John gave full approval to Henry's plans. He knew that, as a third son with two healthy older brothers, Henry would probably never be called upon to rule Portugal. He also knew that Henry had a first-rate mind and boundless energy. Let him use his talents to pursue his own interests—which also happened to be Portugal's interests.

So Henry retired to the windswept promontory at Sagres. Here he would gather the best minds and the best sailors from all over Europe. Together they would

chart the uncharted Atlantic and open up a whole new world of sea travel.

*The rocky coast of Sagres*

It was an ambitious undertaking, but Henry was an ambitious young man. After his part in conquering Ceuta, he was also quite a famous young man. It wasn't hard to lure scholars and mathematicians and mapmakers to Sagres to work with him. Henry was known to be generous, and he paid well for services rendered. More than that, he was guided by genuine scientific fervor. Scholars from all over Europe were drawn to Henry's "school" at Sagres. Nowhere else in Europe could they find such a marvelous opportunity to exchange and explore ideas.

Prince Henry had five main reasons for wanting to explore the African coast by sea. The first was an honest desire to learn more about the world he inhabited. Henry himself defined knowledge as "that from which all good arises." He knew that most sailors sailed for profit. Few would set out on an unknown course just for the sake of finding out what lay beyond the next cape. As a relatively wealthy prince, Henry could afford to explore for the sake of exploration.

Henry's other motives were more practical. His second reason for exploring Africa was commercial— he wanted to know where along Africa's west coast his sailors could safely trade. Were there natural harbors where Portuguese ships could put ashore and trade directly with the Africans?

Going hand in hand with this, Henry wanted to find out more about Islamic strength in Africa. Was all of Africa under Muslim control? If not, how far south did the Moors' power extend?

In wondering about Muslim influence in Africa, Henry also wondered about the presence of any Christians there. For over two hundred years, stories about a legendary Christian king named Prester John had circulated around Europe. (The legend may have grown around either a twelfth-century Ethiopian king or a Chinese prince of the same period.) According to legend, Prester John had successfully fought the Moors and was ready to help European Christians regain the Holy Lands. Prince Henry knew of these legends. He believed that Prester John lived in Ethiopia, and that if he could find him, together they might drive the Infidel out of Africa.

Even if there were no Prester John, Henry felt there should be Christians in Africa. His fifth and final reason for exploring the continent showed true Christian missionary zeal. Henry wished to convert Muslims and pagans alike to Christianity, to "increase the Holy Faith . . . that lost souls might be saved."

His motives established, Henry got down to business. Word went out throughout Europe that the prince was looking for learned men to assist him at Sagres. Mapmakers, navigators, and mathematicians were especially welcome.

The records show that "the Prince devoted great industry and thought to the matter, and at great expense procured the aid of one Master Jacome from Majorca, a man skilled in the art of navigation and in the making of maps and instruments, and certain of the Arab and Jewish mathematicians, to instruct the Portuguese in that science."

Henry had rightly determined that scientific mapmaking, or cartography, was the key to his explorations. Until his time, cartography had been something of a hit-or-miss proposition.

Ancient Greek and Roman geographers had long before established that the earth was round. They had even done a fair job of mapping out the world as far as they knew it. The area around the Mediterranean Sea, Europe, Scandinavia, northern Africa (which the ancients called Libya), Arabia, the Persian Gulf, even the Indian Ocean and parts of Asia—all these had shown up on maps over a thousand years before Prince Henry's time.

What the ancient geographers hadn't known was that a whole Western Hemisphere—North and South America—lay beyond the Atlantic Ocean. No one in Europe or Asia would know that until the late 1400s, after Prince Henry paved the way.

*Greek geographer Eratosthenes*

*Map of the world according to Eratosthenes*

The ancients had also drawn a system of east-west and north-south lines, called longitude and latitude, to help pinpoint precise locations on their maps. One Greek geographer named Eratosthenes had even estimated the distance around the world—its circumference—within 50 miles (80 kilometers) of its actual size.

The problem was that, after the fall of the Roman Empire in A.D. 476, much of the work of these ancient scholars was lost. Wild tribesmen from the north invaded Europe and Asia. They plundered cities, halted

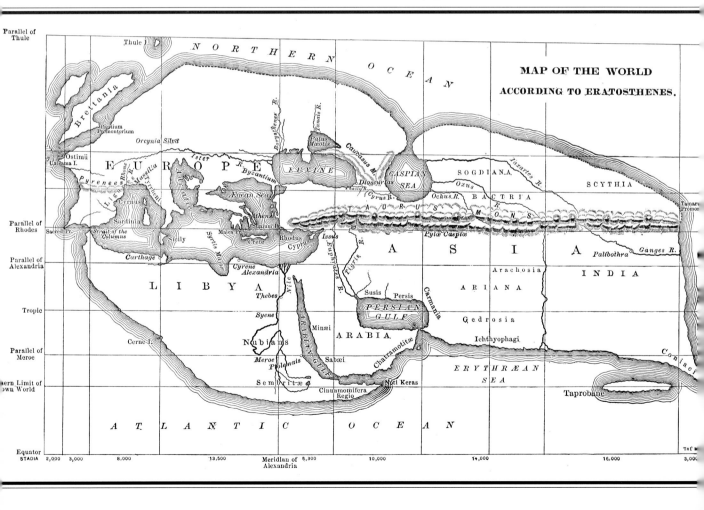

trade, overthrew governments, and in general upset the lives of nobles, scholars, and common people alike.

Then came the rise of Islam in the seventh century A.D. Muslim warriors from the Middle East swarmed out of the desert to invade southern Europe and northern Africa. Taking control of Egypt and the Arabian peninsula, the Moors cut off what little trade still existed between Europe and lands to the east and south.

For hundreds of years, East and West remained isolated from each other. The work of Greek and Roman geographers was lost. Maps began to change. Instead of being factual, they became fanciful and symbolic. They showed the world the way it ought to be—or was feared to be—instead of the way it really was. Seas and continents were much larger or smaller than actual size, to make the world look symmetri-

ly creative. A Muslim trav-
ed that the world ended in
Africa's Cape Bojador. Arab
coast of Africa with writh-
ribly grinning serpents in-
vering over everything was
ready to seize the first hu-
atery domain.
graphers weren't much bet-
as a sort of divine blueprint.
rusalem—or sometimes the
ck in the middle of the world.
h dragons of disbelief crushed

beneath him. Unicorns and other mythical beasts filled in the empty spaces. What medieval mapmakers—Christian or Muslim—didn't know for a fact, they made up.

*Ptolemy at his observatory in Alexandria, Egypt*

These were the maps Prince Henry and his scholars had to work with. Sorting through fact and fancy, they tried to figure out where in the world shorelines and oceans and land masses really *were*. They were helped by the fact that, after being lost for over a thousand years, the maps of the ancient Greek geographers were beginning to resurface.

Unfortunately, the most famous of these maps was the *Geography* of Claudius Ptolemy. Ptolemy, who lived around A.D. 140, knew the world was round. His mathematical approach to cartography, with coordinates for longitude and latitude, helped turn mapmaking into a science.

The problem was, Ptolemy's math calculations weren't always right. Unlike Eratosthenes, Ptolemy underestimated the circumference of the world by some 7,000 miles (11,300 kilometers). He blew up the size of the known land masses, reduced the size of the oceans, left out the unknown Western Hemisphere—and shrank the world by almost a third of its actual size.

Another error on Ptolemy's map had to do with Africa. Ptolemy didn't believe the story about the Phoenicians sailing clear around Africa in 600 B.C. In Ptolemy's world view, the southern tip of Africa stretched eastward until it connected with Asia. If Prince Henry were to rely only on Ptolemy, his ships would never reach India by sailing south and east around Africa.

*Ptolemy's map of the world*

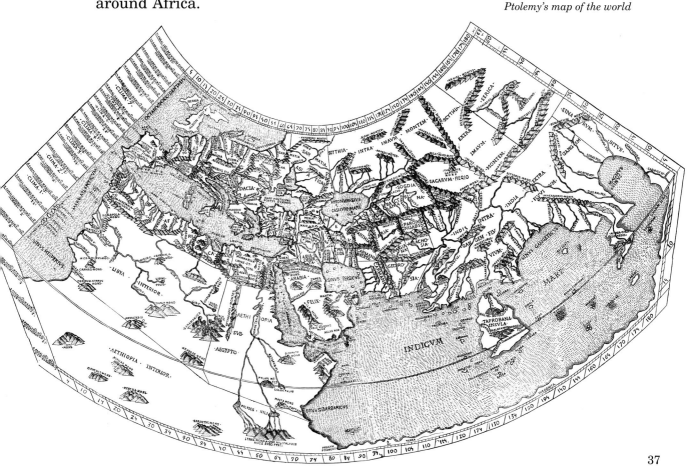

*A Bedouin caravan in North Africa*

Luckily, Henry didn't rely only on Ptolemy. He studied all the ancient and medieval maps he could find. He listened carefully to the Arabs and other travelers who knew the caravan routes of south-central Africa. He became convinced that Africa was a separate continent. He also concluded that it was possible to reach India by going around Africa's southern tip. It was just a question of sailing and charting Africa's coastal waters, cape by cape.

Henry paid special attention to the navigational charts known as *portolani* that made their way to Sagres. These portolani were drawn by Italian seamen, Europe's best sailors. Designed to help real sea captains navigate real coastal waters, the portolani

*Mythical sea beasts*

showed bays and promontories, rocks and reefs, currents and tides. They left out the dragons and demons of Arabic and Christian maps, and instead included realistic drawings of hazards and harbors. The portolani were a great help, as far as they went—only they didn't go far enough. Henry would have to find out for himself most of what lay along Africa's coastline.

So, after he had studied all the maps he could, consulted with all the scholars he could, and read all the travelogues he could, Prince Henry did the only thing left to him. He began sending out ships to discover what really existed beyond the boundaries of the known world.

# Chapter 4
# Isles in the Atlantic

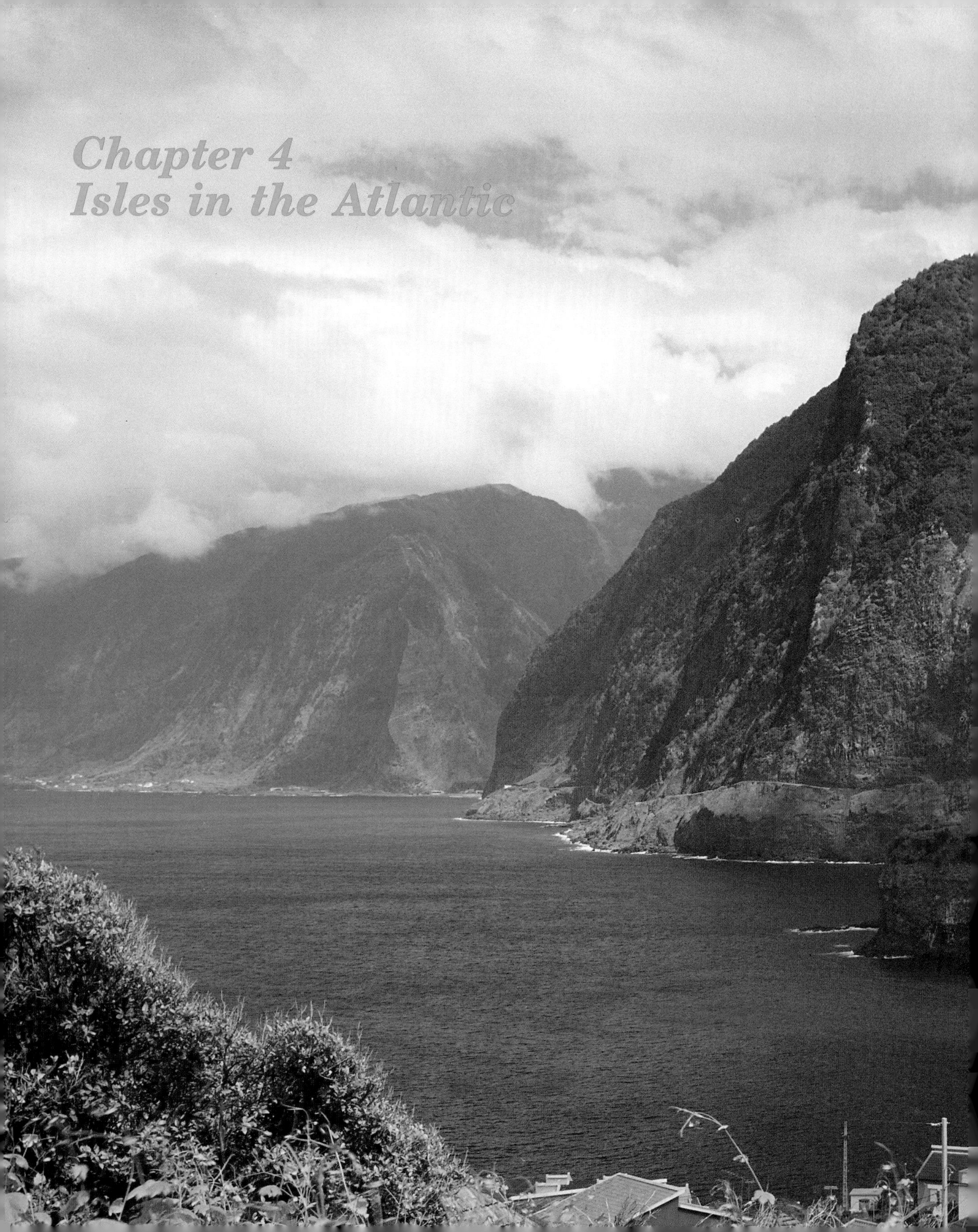

**P**rince Henry may have begun sending ships down the African coast even before the victory at Ceuta. But it was after his return in 1418 that his explorations began in earnest.

Two of the earliest ships Henry dispatched were captained by young nobles of his household, Tristão Vaz Teixeira and João Goncalves Zarco. Henry's instructions were simple enough. He wanted his captains to voyage in search of the land of Guinea, as southwestern Africa was then known.

Vaz Teixeira and Zarco had hardly set sail from Sagres's neighboring port town of Lagos when they were caught in a violent gale. Luckily, their ships didn't break apart, and they were soon washed ashore on an unknown island to the west. Gratefully dubbing the island Santo Porto, the two nobles returned to Sagres to report on their adventure.

Finding islands hadn't been Prince Henry's goal. Still, a discovery was a discovery. He had heard rumors of various islands in the Atlantic. He had seen references to them in maps and travelers' journals. Here was proof that at least one such island truly existed.

Henry carefully charted Santo Porto's location some 700 miles (1,100 kilometers) to the southwest of Portugal. Then he promptly sent Vaz Teixeira and Zarco out again, along with a third captain named Bartholomew Perestrello. Their goal this time was to cultivate Santo Porto with food crops—and they might have succeeded if it hadn't been for the rabbits.

It seems a well-wisher had given Perestrello a pregnant doe rabbit as a going-away present. Once on Santo Porto, this rabbit and her offspring reproduced so rapidly, and gobbled up vegetation so completely, that it was impossible to grow crops. Eventually, Perestrello would succeed in raising cattle on the rabbit-eaten island. But for the present, prospects looked dim. Disgusted, Vaz Teixeira and Zarco returned to Portugal.

Undiscouraged, Prince Henry sent his captains back out to sea. This time, they discovered yet another, even fairer, island beyond Santo Porto. Naming the island Madeira, from the Portuguese word for "wood," they hurried back to Lagos to report their find.

Greatly pleased, Henry granted Zarco and Vaz Teixeira command of the island and began making plans to colonize it. Importing sugar canes from Sicily and grapevines from Crete, he established two cash crops. Along with Madeira's native wood, they eventually brought in quite a healthy income.

The island colony prospered. Balmy weather, softly scented breezes, lush vegetation, sweetly singing birds—Madeira seemed a true paradise on earth. As a visitor some twenty years later wrote, "The whole island is a garden!" Indeed, the first children to be born on Madeira were christened Adam and Eve.

Pleased as he was to have discovered these fruitful islands, Prince Henry didn't forget his real goal. The uncharted coast of Africa still beckoned. Every year, from about 1420 onwards, Henry continued his stubborn quest to round the fabled Cape Bojador, the farthest known point on the west African coast. As soon as spring brought warmer weather and calmer waters to the Atlantic, Henry's ships, with their distinctive white sails and bold red crosses of Christ, headed south into the unknown. Every fall, Henry's captains returned, with stories of marauding Moorish merchant ships and fierce storms at sea—but no mention of Cape Bojador.

Back in Sagres, Henry listened to all that his captains had to say. He insisted that they keep precise logs throughout their journeys. He wanted to know *everything*.

What tides, reefs, and channels had they encountered? What headlands and other natural landmarks did they pass? What were the compass bearings between these landmarks? How strong were the winds, and in which direction did they blow? How many days did they travel before tacking, or zigzagging into the wind? Did they find any natural harbors, or any streams where fresh water could be taken on board? What sea birds did they pass, and in which direction were they flying? How deep was the sea—what *color* was the sea?

All winter, Henry and his mapmakers, astronomers, and mathematicians pored over these logs while cold Atlantic winds howled around them. Slowly, painstakingly, they pieced together the information brought back by Henry's captains. Mile by mile, the map of Africa's coastline began to emerge from the Ocean of Darkness. And every spring, Henry sent his captains back out to sea. He never lost patience with pilots who claimed that high seas and rough weather had kept them from passing Cape Bojador. He listened graciously to the stories of their adventures, rewarded them justly, then immediately sent them out again. As his captains were to discover soon enough, Prince Henry of Portugal didn't take no for an answer!

In 1428, Prince Pedro returned to Portugal from his long travels through Europe. With him he brought a veritable treasure trove of gifts for his younger brother. There was a Latin version of the *Book of Marco Polo*—one of the few copies of that famous Venetian trader's account of his travels through Asia. There was also a fine map of all the parts of the world then known. It had been compiled mainly by Arab traders who had traveled widely throughout the Middle and Far East. Finally, there were the stories Pedro had heard on his journey. These stories, as much as Marco Polo's manuscript and the Moors' map, convinced Henry that he was indeed on the right track in trying to sail southward around Africa's tip.

It may also have been Pedro who first brought Henry information about yet another group of Atlantic islands. Lying some 800 miles (1,300 kilometers) due west of Sagres, these islands occasionally showed up on navigation charts and in travelers' tales. Now Henry decided to find and claim them for Portugal.

*Illustration from the* Book of Marco Polo

It was in 1431 that he sent out Goncalo Velho Cabral, a noble knight and experienced seaman, to find the fabled islands. Setting his sights due west, Cabral and his crew sailed for several days before spotting a barren cluster of rocks rising out of the sea. Seeing no other signs of land, Cabral returned to Lagos to report that no inhabitable island existed.

Prince Henry took the news calmly. Then, as usual, he sent Cabral straight out to sea again. "There is an island there," he assured his captain. "Go back and find it!"

*View of the coast of Ponta Delgada in the Azores*

So Cabral did. First he found the same clump of rocks—now named Formigas—that he had discovered before. Then he set his sights slightly to the southwest. Sure enough, 20 miles (32 kilometers) ahead of him lay a warm, fertile, and definitely habitable island. Planting the Portuguese flag and naming the island Santa Maria, Cabral returned to Portugal for his reward.

Prince Henry was well pleased with his captain's work. Granting him the title of Captain Donatory, he allowed Cabral to recruit settlers and colonize Santa Maria. Over the next twenty-five years, a whole chain of islands would be discovered beyond Santa Maria. Named the Azores, after the Portuguese word for "hawk," they stretched across some 400 miles (650

*View of Ferro Island, as seen off the tip of Porto Santo Island in the Madeiras*

kilometers) of the Atlantic. Prince Henry was pleased to add these profitable islands to Portugal's budding colonial empire. He was especially pleased that his father had lived to see the discovery of Santa Maria. For it was the very next year, in 1433, that good King John of Portugal died. King John was seventy-seven years old. He died peacefully, happy in the knowledge that his country was prosperous and secure in the hands of his five able sons.

With Duarte now crowned King of Portugal in Lisbon, Henry pushed forward with his explorations. He continued to supervise his island colonies of Santo Porto, Madeira, and the Azores. But his real interest, as always, was finding what lay down the coast of Africa, beyond Cape Bojador.

*Native dress of the women of the Azores in the nineteenth century*

Rounding Cape Bojador was still an uphill battle for Henry. His captains were, quite frankly, not as eager as he was to pass that fabled spot. There was nothing beyond that cape, they argued. There were no people, nor any land that would support people. Everywhere was sand and more sand—no water, no trees, no green vegetation of any sort. As for the sea—it was so shallow, and the currents so terrible, that even if a ship *did* pass the cape, it could never return safely home to Portugal.

Fortunately for the rest of the world, Henry was made of sterner stuff than his sea captains. Tall, fair, and well built, the thirty-nine-year-old prince combined a keen mind with a steadfast character and a burning ambition to accomplish great things. If he drove his captains hard, he drove himself still harder. It was well known that Henry frequently worked all through the night, studying his captains' logs and plotting new courses for them. His energy and self-discipline were renowned throughout Europe, where he had the reputation for making the impossible seem downright easy.

Finally, in 1434, Prince Henry's hard work was rewarded. One of his captains, a nobleman named Gil Eannes, had just returned from an African sea voyage. Eannes rattled off the usual excuses for not rounding Cape Bojador.

Henry listened patiently, then chided Eannes for behaving like a novice captain who didn't know how to use a compass or a sailing chart.

"Go forth again," Prince Henry scolded. "Make your voyage straight away. Heed nothing else but passing Cape Bojador, and you will have both honor and reward."

*Gil Eannes*

By all accounts, Prince Henry was a man of very great authority. When he spoke, people listened. It was clear to Gil Eannes that this time his prince meant business. There were to be no more excuses.

Gil Eannes set sail once again. As Cape Bojador came into view, he took a deep breath and told his men to set their sails westward. Making a wide turn to avoid the shallows and reefs near the shore, Eannes came back inland to discover that he had, indeed, put the dreaded cape behind him.

It was almost too easy. There were no sea monsters, no raging whirlpools, no magnetic rocks to pull the fittings out of the ship. There was just desert coastline and sea, as there had been for miles before.

Greatly relieved, Eannes sailed on for a few more miles, then put ashore in a small boat. The bare Saharan sands offered no signs of human life. But Eannes did collect a few of the windswept plants known in Portugal as St. Mary's Roses to carry home to Prince Henry.

Gil Eannes was given a hero's welcome when he was back in Sagres. "For, although the matter was a small one in itself, yet on account of its daring it was reckoned great."

Urged on by his prince, Gil Eannes had broken the barrier of fear and superstition that had long surrounded Cape Bojador. The coast of Africa was now officially open for exploration.

Prince Henry pressed on with no delay. In 1435 he sent Gil Eannes back out to sea, this time with a second ship, captained by Afonso Goncalves Baldaia. The two vessels worked their way down the coast 150 miles (240 kilometers) past Bojador. Going ashore, the landing party found tracks of men and camels on the sandy beach.

Excitedly, Eannes and Baldaia returned home to tell Prince Henry about their find. This was the first proof that the lands Henry was so interested in were, in fact, habitable.

But who were the inhabitants? Could Henry's captains have found Prester John's Christian kingdom? Or were the Africans along this coast heathens, waiting to receive the word of Christ and so be saved for Christendom?

*Sand dunes of the Sahara*

Religious matters aside, was it possible that the tracks belonged to Arab traders?

Henry needed to know. He needed to talk to an African, to find out for himself the answer to these and his many other questions. He sent Baldaia out in another ship, back down the coast. Baldaia's orders were simple and specific—to bring back a native inhabitant for Henry to question at Sagres.

Baldaia sailed nearly 200 miles (320 kilometers) farther down the coast than he had on his previous voyage. Landing, he sent two young squires on horseback to search out local inhabitants. The two came back with tales of a skirmish, in which a group of startled Africans had fought them off with rocks and stones.

The next day Baldaia went farther inland, this time with more men. Again, they were unable to take any captives.

So it was back to sea. This time Baldaia didn't head immediately home to Portugal. Instead, he continued south another 150 miles (240 kilometers) down the coast.

Finding what seemed to be the mouth of a large river (but which turned out to be merely a deep and narrow inlet), he put ashore a landing party and dubbed the spot Río de Oro, River of Gold.

There wasn't much that was golden about the spot. Arid and deserted, it had no inhabitants for Baldaia to take home to Henry.

Baldaia did find an abundance of sea lions, though—which were promptly killed and skinned— and a curiously woven fishnet lying abandoned on the beach. Satisfying themselves with these small treasures, Baldaia and his men sailed for home.

# Chapter 5
# Tragedy at Tangier

**B**ack at Sagres, Prince Henry met Baldaia with his usual courtesy, but perhaps with a little less than his customary enthusiasm. If Henry seemed preoccupied that summer of 1436, there were reasons. For once, he had something more important on his mind than voyages of exploration.

This "something" was another chance to battle the Moors on their own turf. For years, Henry had urged his father to attack Ceuta's neighboring city of Tangier. Like Ceuta, Tangier was a Muslim stronghold and therefore an honorable target for a good Christian knight. Tangier also had an excellent harbor on the Atlantic side of the Strait of Gibraltar. It would be enormously convenient if Portugal controlled such a strategically placed harbor.

King John had always turned a deaf ear to Henry's entreaties about taking Tangier. He was growing old, he had spent much of his youth in battle, and he was delighted to be ruling a peaceable kingdom. Besides, Ceuta had turned out to be an expensive victory for Portugal. Maintaining another garrison in Tangier would cost the kingdom too much.

Now King John was dead. With Duarte on the throne, Henry brought up the subject of Tangier again. His brother seemed to like Henry's idea of an attack. But if Duarte listened to Henry with one ear, he listened to Pedro with the other. And Pedro was adamantly opposed to the scheme. There was plenty to attend to at home without looking for trouble abroad.

Henry turned to his other brothers for support. Prince John, the middle brother, was no help at all. A thoughtful young man, Prince John offered convincing arguments both for making war and for staying peacefully at home. Logically, he considered war with the Infidel from two points of view, that of honor and that of common sense. Then, having presented both sides of the argument, he sat down with a nod in King Duarte's direction. "I leave the decision to you," he finished maddeningly.

Henry's most important ally turned out to be his youngest brother, Fernando. Fernando had been only eleven when his older brothers stormed Ceuta. Now he, too, wished to earn his knighthood in honorable battle. Tangier seemed the obvious place.

After a year of discussion, debate, and indecision, King Duarte made up his mind. Portugal would attack the Muslim city of Tangier in the fall of 1437. Prince Henry would lead the Portuguese army, with Fernando at his side.

It was a tragic decision. Unlike the campaign for Ceuta, this expedition was poorly planned, poorly manned, and poorly executed. Instead of overwhelming the Moors at Tangier, Prince Henry and his troops were decisively defeated. As a soldier in Ceuta, Henry had been brave, reckless, and a hero. As a commander in Tangier, he was brave, reckless, and incompetent.

*Moroccan landscape*

He failed to judge his enemy's strength adequately. He allowed his escape route to the sea to be cut off. Finally, with his troops dying of thirst in the blazing desert sun, he was forced to sign a humiliating surrender.

The terms of the surrender were truly painful. In return for safe passage back to their ships, the Portuguese had to leave all their weapons on the battlefield, return Ceuta to the Moors, and promise not to fight against Muslims for a hundred years. As a guarantee of their good faith, one of the Portuguese princes, Henry or Fernando, would have to stay in Tangier until Ceuta was surrendered.

Both Henry and Fernando immediately volunteered to remain hostage. But Henry's soldiers and advisors would not hear of their commander-in-chief giving himself up. At last, sick at heart, Henry agreed to let Fernando stay in his place. It would only be a matter of weeks, he assured himself, before his brother would be safely ransomed.

But this was not to be. The Moors didn't honor their promise to let Henry and his troops return safely to their ships. Instead, the Portuguese had to fight their own desperate way to the beach. Back in Lisbon,

*Ceuta, as seen across the Strait of Gibraltar*

the king's advisors used this as an excuse not to give up Ceuta. Fernando must be released without the surrender of Ceuta, they insisted. Think of Portugal's disgrace in the eyes of Europe if they gave up what had been so gloriously won just twenty years earlier!

Even Henry eventually came to agree that Ceuta must not given back to the Moors. Winning the city had been a holy victory for Christ. It was not in a mere mortal's power to surrender what belonged to God. If Fernando could not be ransomed by exchanging other hostages, he, Henry, would lead another military attack on Tangier. Prince Pedro violently disagreed with his brother. Another military expedition would be suicidal, and the Moors had made it clear they weren't interested in any exchange of hostages. As for surrendering Ceuta—well, in Pedro's mind, Ceuta had never been anything but a drain on Portugal's coffers. It would be a relief to give it up.

Poor King Duarte wavered between his two strong-minded brothers. Fernando was dearly beloved by the king. The whole Tangier expedition had been planned with his honor and glory in mind. To think of him languishing in some dark Moorish prison was unbearable. But to surrender Ceuta seemed equally unthinkable. Night after night, Duarte agonized over the problem.

In the end, the dilemma proved too much for the king. A letter from Fernando, describing his sufferings, helped bring about Duarte's physical collapse. Feverish and troubled, King Duarte died on September 9, 1438. The cause of death given by his doctors was, "An unparalleled sorrow, and acute distress resulting from the misfortunes of Tangier." With his last breath, King Duarte blamed himself for those misfortunes.

*Queen Leonor*

With King Duarte's death, the question of Fernando's release became secondary. The real question, and the problem threatening to push Portugal into civil war, was who would now rule the country. Duarte's eldest son and successor to the throne was a child of six. Clearly, young Afonso would need a regent to aid him in his royal duties. The question was—should that regent be his mother the queen, or his uncle, Prince Pedro?

The court and population of Portugal were bitterly divided over this issue. For three years the controversy raged. Called on as a peacemaker, Prince Henry took a leading role in working out various compromises. When the dust finally cleared in 1441, Queen Leonor had exiled herself to Spain in a proud fury, leaving young King Afonso in the sole charge of his Uncle Pedro.

Meanwhile, Fernando still languished in prison. King Duarte's will left specific instructions that Ceuta was to be surrendered for his brother's release, but by now the Moors weren't interested in freeing the young prince. Alone, in chains, sick in body and soul, Fernando finally died in captivity in 1443. The tragedy of Tangier was complete. It was the bitterest blow Prince Henry of Portugal was ever to know.

*Fernando, held prisoner by the Moors*

# Chapter 6
# On the Rocks of Sagres

After Tangier, Prince Henry became a virtual recluse in his windswept haven at Sagres. He had never had much to do with the pomp and circumstance of court life. A member of the holy Order of Christ, he had long ago adopted a chaste and sober life-style. Now he rarely showed his face in public.

If Lisbon didn't benefit from Prince Henry's presence, Sagres certainly did. As the years passed, the *Vila do Infante*, City of the Prince, became renowned throughout Europe. There was the chapel Henry had built, along with the hospital, the warehouse, and the fortress. There was a palace for himself, with a library to hold his huge collection of books and maps, as well as inns and lodges for visiting scholars and sailors. Lastly, and perhaps most important, there was the observatory—the first ever built on European soil. Here, in the company of his astronomers and mathematicians, Henry studied the night sky for hours on end, looking for clues to guide his sailors into unknown seas.

In this and many other ways Henry showed himself to be ahead of his time. The heavens had always been important in medieval thought. But others looked to the stars for mystical signs and signals, while Henry's interest was purely practical. Studying the movement of the stars could help his sailors determine time, and therefore position, when they were far out to sea.

Measuring time was always a problem for early sailors. Medieval Europe had clocks, but they were far too fragile and expensive to take on board ships. Hourglasses were used instead. Hour after hour, they were

*An early method of navigation—taking a sighting of the North Star using a cross staff*

watched and turned by cabin boys whose only job was to log the rotations of these clocks.

Why was it so important to measure time accurately? One way ship captains measured how fast and far they were traveling was by use of a logline. A series of knots was tied in a line or rope attached to a small log. As a seaman released this line into the water, the speed at which the knots slipped through his fingers gave the speed of the ship. This is where the nautical measure of "knots" came from. For the logline to be accurate, the seamen had to be able to accurately estimate time. Woe be it to the cabin boy who forgot to log an hourglass rotation—or who warmed the sand to make it flow faster, and hence shorten his watch! Then, too, seamen were beginning to read the position of the stars to determine their longitude. To do this accurately, they needed to mark the precise time of each of their readings. Without accurate clocks, with balance wheels and hairsprings, measuring longitude at sea was practically impossible.

So Henry was interested in better, more accurate ways of measuring time. He was also concerned with how to measure distance and direction. Medieval sailors knew about compasses, with their needles always pointing north. But magnetism was only poorly understood five hundred years ago. Many seamen still regarded compasses with superstition and distrust.

Not Henry. He insisted that all his vessels carry compasses to keep them on a straight course when out of sight of land. Back at Sagres, he and his scholars worked hard to understand exactly how a compass worked and to improve its reliability. Henry even had a huge compass face built into the courtyard at Sagres to help train his mariners.

*A Portuguese astrolabe used as a navigational device in the fifteenth century*

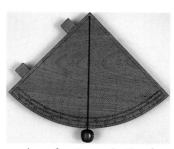

*A quadrant, a navigational instrument in Portugal's Marine Museum*

Henry also encouraged his captains to carry an instrument known as the astrolabe. Astrolabes were used to measure the angle of the sun and stars from the horizon. Astronomers had long relied on these instruments to determine latitude, or distances north or south of the equator. But like clocks, astrolabes were too delicate to take on board small ships. Henry and his astronomers devised a simplified version for ship captains to carry.

Henry then encouraged his pilots to take their bearings from dry land whenever possible, instead of from the rolling deck of a ship. As Henry well knew—and as his pilots were beginning to find out—accuracy was everything when charting new lands.

*The astrolabe of Philip II of Spain*

Developing and improving navigational tools was just one of the innovations to come out of Henry's "school" at Sagres. Another was Henry's insistence that his pilots keep accurate records of each of their expeditions. These pilots' logs became invaluable tools as, inch by inch, Henry's cartographers mapped out the unfamiliar African coastline.

*Model of a Portuguese ship known as a carraca*

Henry also worked hard on improving the design of his ships at Sagres. The first ships he sent out were either *barcas* or *barinels*. Barcas were small, square-sailed ships that carried a crew of about twenty. They sailed well with the wind, but traveling into the wind was a slow, laborious process. Barinels relied on oarsmen as well as a square sail, but again, rowing into the wind was exhausting work.

As Henry well knew, the prevailing winds along the African coast were northwesterlies—winds blowing from the northwest. That meant that his ships' return journeys were almost always spent sailing into the wind. With a crew that was already tired from weeks at sea, and supplies of fresh food and water running low, too long a return journey could spell disaster for an entire expedition. It was vital that Henry and his shipbuilders come up with a better boat design.

So they did. From the visitors at Sagres, Henry had learned of the Arab ships known as *caravos*. Caravos were large, sturdy ships able to carry a large crew and a great deal of cargo. Instead of square sails, caravos had triangular, slanting sails known as lateens. These lateen sails made it easier for the ships to sail into the wind. Henry also knew of the ships of northern Portugal, called *caravelas*. Small, swift, and easy to steer, caravelas also used lateen sails.

*A Portuguese caravela, with slanting lateen salis*

Henry and his shipbuilders put their heads together. Combining the size and cargo capacity of the caravos with the speed and agility of the caravelas, they designed a compact and maneuverable vessel called the caravel. The caravel had three masts, each with its own triangular-shaped lateen sail. Because of these sails and the design of the hull, caravels could sail easily and smoothly into the wind. They could also sail in shallower waters than barcas. This proved invaluable in exploring Africa's coastal and inshore waters. And, unlike the barcas, caravels could be easily beached and heeled over for repairs.

All of these improvements meant that Henry's seamen could make quicker, safer, more comfortable voyages than ever before. As one enthusiastic captain exclaimed, "Caravels are the best ships that sail the sea, and there is nowhere impossible for them to navigate!"

Even on a caravel, however, early ocean travel was primitive. The captain had a small covered cabin, but crew members lived and worked on the open deck—except in the worst weather, when they could take shelter in the cramped cargo hold. Food was monotonous—barrels of salted meat, dried fish, lemons, and olives. Sometimes there was cheese, and always there were the hard, dry sea biscuits that were specially baked in the royal ovens at Lisbon. Rice and beans were fine—as long as the supply of cooking water held out—and of course garlic was good for flavoring. There was usually an abundance of wine to wash down the salty provisions, but fresh drinking water was hard to come by on the arid Sahara coast. Still, plenty of mariners were willing to put up with primitive living conditions in exchange for adventure and profit. It

*Portrait of Prince Henry*

was well known that Prince Henry generously rewarded those who sailed for him. And Henry was able to inspire his seamen to do more than even they thought possible.

This was shown vividly on the voyage taken in 1441 by a young sea captain named Antao Conçalves. Because Conçalves was young and rather inexperienced, Henry assigned him a simple task. He was to sail to Baldaia's Río de Oro and collect the skins and oil of the sea lions that lived there.

Conçalves did as he was told. Then, his mission completed, the young seaman felt the itch to accomplish bigger and better things. Just think how pleased his prince would be if, besides this "petty merchandise," Conçalves were to bring home to Henry the first African captive!

Conçalves laid his plans carefully. When night fell, he and nine of his men left their ship and took a hot and thirsty hike inland through the desert. More by luck than strategy, they happened on a Arab man and a black woman. They promptly ambushed the two and brought them back to the ship.

They had hardly boarded the ship when they saw another vessel approaching from the north. Bearing Henry's distinctive red cross on its sails, this ship proved to be a caravel (the first caravel on record), captained by one Nuno Tristão. Tristão had left Lagos shortly after Conçalves had. His orders had been to sail farther than any captain before him and to bring back a captive for Henry to question. To help him in his mission, Tristão had a Moor on board to serve as interpreter.

Now here was young Conçalves with not one, but two Africans to question. Greatly pleased, Tristão brought out his interpreter. Unfortunately, the Moor couldn't understand a single word spoken by the two captives.

Undaunted, Tristão proposed another raiding party. In this nighttime ambush, the Portuguese killed four natives and captured ten. One of the ten, a minor chief named Adahu, spoke Arabic. Delighted, Tristão decided to send Adahu back to Portugal with Conçalves. Tristão himself would continue exploring down the African coast.

But first Tristão had an important ceremony to perform. On a sandy, almost deserted beach, he knighted Antao Conçalves, in recognition of his service to his prince and his country. Chivalric valor—even if it only meant capturing a few frightened, unarmed African natives—must be rewarded according to the medieval code of honor. While Conçalves took Adahu back to Sagres, Nuno Tristão continued southward as far as a cape of white cliffs he named Cape Blanco. Though he took no other captives, Tristão accomplished a significant feat. Noting that his caravel needed repairs, he beached the ship, heeled it over on its side, mended it, and then cast out to sea again.

His crew marveled at Tristão's boldness—as well they ought. Such actions would have been impossible with a barca or a barinel, both of which needed a deep harbor and heavy equipment to make repairs. Never before had a captain felt confident enough to beach his ship on unfamiliar African shores, make repairs, and then set out to sea again. It was clear proof of the caravel's adaptability and ease of handling.

Back at Sagres, Henry was eagerly questioning Adahu. From the Moor, Henry heard first-hand accounts of caravans with as many as three hundred gold-laden camels from the south. He heard stories of the rich and fabled city of Timbuktu, "meeting place of the camel and the canoe." He learned how mighty rivers like the Senegal and the Gambia flowed westward into the Atlantic and served as highways into the interior.

Most interesting were Adahu's descriptions of the land of Guinea, that green and fertile country south of the great Sahara Desert. While the trade routes of the Sahara belonged to the Moors, Guinea lay outside of

*Henry hoped to link his expeditions with those of the Crusaders, who tried to win the Holy Land back from the Moors. This picture shows fourteenth-century Crusaders embarking on a mission.*

Muslim control. The black kings of Guinea ruled their own kingdoms. They could trade directly with Portugal—and one of them might be Prester John.

It was all Henry needed to hear. He immediately sent a group of diplomats to Pope Eugene IV. Henry had several requests for the Pope. First, he wanted all new lands beyond Cape Bojador to belong to Portugal. (By medieval law, the Pope decided who would rule over any newly found and unoccupied land. Unoccupied, that is, by Christians—the rights of heathens and infidels weren't much considered.) Next, he requested that his own Order of Christ have spiritual rule over these new lands and any converts made there. Finally, Henry asked that any explorers who died on his expeditions be considered holy Christian crusaders, with full forgiveness of their sins.

The Pope lost no time granting all of Henry's requests. Henry's brother, the regent Prince Pedro, added his stamp of approval, too. By royal proclamation, Henry was allowed one-fifth of any profit from African explorations—a right normally belonging to the king. Pedro also recognized how much of his own money Henry had already spent on his expeditions. To help his brother earn back some of his expenses, Pedro commanded that "henceforth no one might sail down the African coast without permission from the Prince Navigator."

For all practical purposes, Africa now belonged to Prince Henry of Portugal. After nearly twenty years of lonely vigilance on the rocks of Sagres, Henry was finally beginning to reap his reward.

*Elmina Castle, a Portuguese stronghold in West Africa*

# Chapter 7
# Another Alexander

With the backing of the Pope and the regent Prince Pedro, Henry pushed full steam ahead on his expeditions. Having learned all he could from Adahu, he graciously sent the Moor back to his African homeland. Adahu assured Henry that his people would be happy to pay ransom for his return. There would also be a healthy ransom for two of the other captives taken along the Río de Oro.

Prince Henry had Antao Gonçalves, who had captured Adahu, return him in 1443. As it turned out, no ransom was ever collected for Adahu. But the two other Arab captives were exchanged for ten black Africans, some gold dust, a leather shield, and an abundance of ostrich eggs—three of which, it is said, Henry cooked and ate back in Sagres.

It was the gold dust that most interested Henry and the rest of the world, however. Was Portugal finally going to break the Moors' monopoly on the priceless gold trade?

Henry lost no time finding out. Nuno Tristão was the next Portuguese captain to set sail, again in his favorite ship, the caravel. Tristão was Henry's kind of sea captain. Each voyage took him little farther than the one before, and he never failed to return with detailed logbooks and fresh observations.

On this trip, Tristão sailed past the white cliffs he had already named Cape Blanco, some 320 miles (515 kilometers) beyond the once-dreaded Cape Bojador. Continuing south, he dropped anchor in a small inlet he named Arguim Bay. When two canoes of natives paddled out to investigate the ship, Tristão was puzzled. Because of the natives' unique method of paddling with their legs, the Portuguese at first thought they were giant birds skimming the water. But as soon as they saw they were men, Tristão and his sailors brightened. Here was a chance to capture more natives for Prince Henry.

This was to become a common reaction for the exploring Portuguese captains. At first, they took captives back to Sagres for Henry to question. As explorers of an unknown continent, the Portuguese relied on information from natives to help them on their way. Later, the Portuguese took captives to sell as slaves. For the next four hundred years, slavery was the dark side of exploration—for Portugal and for other European countries as well.

It was in this very Arguim Bay that Henry would build, in 1448, an armed fort to handle Portugal's growing gold and slave trade along the African coast.

This small trading post would mark the beginning of the vast colonial empires of the Portuguese, Dutch, English, French, and Spanish all around the world.

By now, Europe was beginning to notice Henry's activities. For years, his voyages had been met with amused tolerance: a prince needs something to keep himself busy, after all. Some viewed him with outright scorn. All that toil and expense, and for what? It was mere foolishness—or, worse, an unforgivable drain on Portugal's finances. But now that Henry's voyages were beginning to bear fruit, people all over Europe began to sing a different tune. Why, this prince was greater than any explorer who had ever lived.

*A slave shed built by African slave traders*

*Early map of West Africa showing the Gambia and Senegal rivers*

Henry was even greater than Alexander, that fabled ancient explorer who was said to have wept when there were no more worlds for him to conquer! The next sailing ships to wear Henry's red Cross of Christ were outfitted by a private citizen named Lancarote. With Henry's permission, Lancarote sent six caravels down the African coast. His reasons were purely commercial: this was a slaving expedition. One of the ships was captained by Gil Eannes, the man who had first rounded Cape Bojador. When the ships returned

*Victims of Portuguese slave hunters*

in the summer of 1444, they carried over two hundred African captives. On August 8, 1444, the town of Lagos held its first slave auction.

It wasn't a pretty sight. Children were torn from their mothers' arms; husbands and wives were cruelly separated. Crying out to each other in grief-stricken terror, the captives were helpless to stop what was happening to them. Although the Portuguese couldn't understand the Africans' language, their anguish was plain enough.

As one chronicler of the time noted uncomfortably, "It was impossible to effect this separation without extreme pain." Prince Henry observed this heartbreaking scene from horseback. According to Prince Pedro's royal decree, one-fifth of the captives belonged to him. Henry showed no interest in claiming any slaves, however—in fact, he gave away on the spot the forty-six Africans that were his due. Rather than feeling pain, Henry is said to have felt "unspeakable satisfaction" at the auction. It was thanks to his efforts that these "heathen" African souls could now be converted to Christianity and saved for all eternity.

It is difficult today to understand Prince Henry's attitude. True, he had no desire to profit from the slave auction. But neither did he show any compassion for the captives' terrible suffering. Could he really have rejoiced for the saving of their souls, now that they were in a good Christian country?

It's possible that he could. For devout Christians of the time, non-believers were truly doomed people. A little unhappiness in this world was nothing compared to the bliss of eternal salvation. Saving "lost" heathen souls—and many African slaves did become Christians while living in Portugal—was truly a holy undertaking. Then, too, the slave trade was nothing new to Henry and others of his time. Slavery had flourished during the ancient Roman Empire, and it continued to flourish in Africa during Henry's lifetime. Since so many Africans would end up as slaves anyway, surely it was better that they be sold to Christians than to the dreaded Infidel. And the fact was, Portuguese economics made slavery attractive. Portugal had always been a small country. Plagues and wars over the past hundred years had reduced

*An African slave market*

the population even more. Both at home and in Prince Henry's new colonies, the Portuguese could use some free labor.

Prince Henry may have had another reason for turning a blind eye to the African slave trade. The more profits his expeditions produced, the easier it would be to recruit eager captains and crews. Henry himself may have been interested in discovery for discovery's sake. But many of his mariners had greedier motives.

However Henry may have justified his actions, the slave-auction scene that day at Lagos would be repeated again and again throughout the European Age of Discovery. Introducing Europe to the slave trade was the least admirable of Prince Henry's many legacies.

To Henry's credit, he did try to discourage the slave raiding parties that some of his captains favored. Henry preferred to deal peaceably with Africa's inhabitants. It was better for trade and better for Christian conversions. His mariners were permitted to barter for slaves already captured by Moors or other Africans. But they were strictly forbidden to raid peaceful villages during a voyage of exploration.

Unfortunately, some of Henry's captains ignored their prince's orders. One such captain was a young squire named Goncalo de Cintra. Cintra set sail in 1445, the year after the Lagos slave auction. His orders were to go straight down the African coast, beyond Arguim Bay, without stopping for anything. Cintra chose to flaunt those orders. He was an ambitious man and a greedy one. He knew what riches a cargo full of slaves could bring him. Anchoring his boat in Arguim Bay, Cintra ignored his crew's protests and went ashore in search of captives.

It was a disastrous decision. Ambushed by some two hundred native inhabitants, Cintra and seven of his men were quickly overwhelmed and killed. They were the first of Henry's explorers to die a violent death while on a voyage of exploration.

Fortunately, not all of Henry's adventurers were so greedy. In 1445, the same year that Cintra was killed, a young squire named João Fernandes set out on a unique expedition. Knowing his prince's desire to learn more about Africa, Fernandes volunteered to spend an entire winter in that continent's interior. Dropped off near the Río de Oro, Fernandes came back the next year with incredible stories.

Fernandes had spent most of the winter traveling with Muslim nomad shepherds through the wastes of the Sahara Desert. He had learned how desert dwellers were guided by winds and stars and the migration of birds, just as sailors were at sea. He had seen ostriches and antelope and gazelles, and the same swallows that spent their summers in Portugal. Most exciting of all, Fernandes had learned more of that mysterious land of Guinea, where storks migrated in winter, and where there was "gold in great abundance." Prince Henry was determined to find this rich and bounteous land of Guinea. In 1445, a captain named Diníz Dias, who was described as "a man who wished to see new things," sailed even farther south. He sailed beyond the arid Sahara to the mouth of the Senegal River at Cape Verde. Dias came back to Sagres with reports of a green land populated by peaceful people and tame cattle. Dias was generously rewarded by Prince Henry—the more so because he hadn't interrupted his voyage for slave raids.

Henry had no lack of eager captains these days. Lagos was crowded with caravels being outfitted and crews recruited for expeditions to the Guinea coast. In August of 1445, some twenty-six ships set sail for Arguim Bay alone.

Not all of the ships were financed by Prince Henry. Now that riches—mainly in the form of slaves—were being brought back from Africa, private individuals were paying for their own expeditions. Even with the one-fifth share owed to Prince Henry, an African slaving ship was quite a money maker.

All this interest in Africa was a mixed blessing for Prince Henry. On the one hand, he welcomed the adventurous mariners who volunteered for his voyages. On the other hand, mere slaving expeditions were not what he had in mind. Henry still wanted to set up peaceful trading relations with the people of Guinea. Wherever possible, he wanted to convert the Africans to Christianity, not subject them to slavery. And he never lost sight of his goal to sail clear around Africa to the wealth of the Indies.

Unfortunately, news of the Portuguese slave missions was spreading down the African coast. The inhabitants of Guinea quickly learned to fear and resist the ships with white sails and red crosses. This was

*Mindelo on Sao Vicente, among the Cape Verde Islands*

tragically illustrated in the last voyage of Nuno Tristão, a fateful journey that took place in 1446.

One of Prince Henry's most favored pilots, Tristão was the discoverer of Cape Blanco, the discoverer of Arguim Bay, and the first captain of a caravel. This time, as usual, he was sailing farther than any Portuguese had ever gone before. He sailed beyond Cape Verde, past the palm-fringed Cape of the Masts, all the way to the mouth of the great Gambia River. Nuno Tristão was now a thousand miles (1,600 kilometers) past Cape Bojador and two thousand miles from Portugal. He was well into the green and fertile land of Guinea. Tristão decided to take two of the ship's smaller boats inland up the great green river he had found. Surely there must be a village upstream, where he could peaceably question the inhabitants about the nature of their land.

There was a village, and there were inhabitants. But these villagers had heard all they needed to know about white men in great sailing vessels. As Tristão and his crew paddled quietly into the lush green rain forest, the villagers closed in around them. Suddenly, twelve canoes carrying eighty warriors emerged from the dense foliage. A shower of arrows—poisoned arrows—rained down on the Portuguese.

Of the twenty-two men in Tristão's boats, four were dead before they even reached their caravel and sixteen more were dying. The shower of arrows followed the survivors on board. Frantically, the Portuguese cut loose their anchors and left the small boats behind. Despite their haste, two of the seven sailors who had remained on the caravel were also hit. In all, twenty-two men were killed, and two more were wounded so badly that they lay hopelessly ill for weeks.

*The Hombori Mountains of western Africa*

The situation on board was truly desperate. There were only five able-bodied survivors: a young African captive, two Portuguese boys who had attended the dead knights, one very young sailor, and an even younger "boy of the Prince's household" named Aires Tinoco. It was Aires Tinoco who proved to be the hero of the day. The young sailor confessed that he could only follow directions and could not direct the caravel himself, but he showed true initiative. His years in Prince Henry's household had been put to good use. He had learned to read and write and had listened carefully to all the talk about sailing and navigation.

*The fort of Pau da Bandeira at Lagos, Portugal*

Now, taking his courage in his hands, he set a course north by east, letting the sun guide him by day and the North Star by night. For two months the sad caravel limped along, never once catching sight of land. Finally, Tinoco's labors were rewarded. Another ship appeared over the horizon—a friendly ship whose captain told them they were directly off the coast of Portugal. Gratefully, Tinoco turned eastward and docked at Lagos. "And thence they went to the Prince to tell him of the tragical fortune of their voyage, and laid before him the multitude of arrows by which their companions had died."

**P**rince Henry was greatly moved when Aires Tinoco and his crewmates returned to Sagres to tell their woeful tale. He rewarded the survivors, gave pensions to the wives and children of those who had died—then turned his mind to matters of state. Once again, the affairs of the royal court at Lisbon were demanding Henry's attention.

All was not well in Portugal in 1448. For six years, from 1441 until 1447, Prince Pedro had governed the country well as regent for his young nephew King Afonso. He had worked hard to preserve Portugal's peace and prosperity and had generously supported Henry's African expeditions.

Throughout these years, Pedro had behaved like a kind and loving father to the young king. In fact, when Afonso turned fourteen in 1446 and was officially installed as King Afonso V, he begged his uncle to stay on as regent and help govern the kingdom.

Prince Pedro was happy to do as his young nephew wished. But not everyone at the Lisbon court was so pleased. Ever since the quarrel over who would be regent in 1438, there had been a group of nobles who resented Pedro's influence over Afonso. There was little they could do while the king was still a child.

Once King Afonso came of age, however, these nobles tried to turn the boy against his uncle. Their goal was to strip Prince Pedro of all authority at the court. Why would anyone bear such a grudge against the hardworking Prince Pedro?

The roots of the quarrel went back many years, to the young manhood of Pedro's father, King John. Before King John married Queen Philippa, he had fathered two illegitimate children, Afonso and Beatriz. Beatriz left Portugal at an early age to marry an English nobleman. Afonso traveled throughout Europe for several years and then returned to Portugal as the Count of Barcelos. For years he had jealously followed the careers of his five younger half-brothers. He grew to be a bitter man. He had not softened even when Prince Pedro made him Duke of Braganza. Now he was determined that he and his sons should take Prince Pedro's place at court.

So the Duke of Braganza set about poisoning young King Afonso's mind against his uncle. Among other charges, the duke suggested that Pedro had had a hand in the death of Afonso's mother, Queen Leonor. That was an outright lie—as were the duke's other

*Afonso, Duke of Braganza*

charges—but the young king couldn't help wondering. Queen Leonor *had* died abroad, in mysterious circumstances. Troubled and confused, King Afonso dismissed Pedro as regent and stripped him of his power at court.

Saddened, Prince Pedro returned to his private estate near the city of Coimbra. Even here, he continued to be harassed by the Duke of Braganza and his allies. Finally, Prince Henry had to leave Sagres to come to his brother's defense.

*Painting by Nuno Goncalves showing Afonso (kneeling), Henry (standing beside him), and many other notable political and spiritual leaders of the time*

Henry was received coolly at the court in Lisbon. Unable to change King Afonso's mind, Henry called upon a knight named Alvara Vaz de Almada for support. A national hero, Alvara Vaz was famous throughout all of Europe for his knightly courage and honor. Henry was sure that this noble crusader could talk some sense into King Afonso, so he retired again to Sagres.

But even Alvara Vaz was no match for the Duke of Braganza. As the weeks went on, Pedro's situation became more and more dangerous. While Henry advised patience, King Afonso authorized the Duke of Braganza to organize an army to march on Prince Pedro's estate. By now events were truly desperate.

*Henry dressed according to his strong religious sentiments*

Even King Afonso's beloved young bride—who happened to be Prince Pedro's own daughter—was unable to save her father's life. On May 20, 1449, Prince Pedro was killed in armed battle with the king's forces.

It was a black moment in Portugal's history. At the court in Lisbon, Prince Henry was stunned and sickened by Pedro's death. Of King John and Queen Philippa's five sons, Henry was now the only one left. Duarte had died of grief in 1438. Prince John had succumbed to a long illness in 1442. Fernando had perished in his Moorish prison in 1443. Now Prince Pedro was dead. Queen Philippa's handful of arrows was reduced to one.

Wishing to leave Portugal—and, perhaps, to redeem himself in holy battle against the Infidel—Henry asked King Afonso's permission to go to Ceuta. Permission was denied. Disheartened, Henry returned to his sanctuary at Sagres.

As always, hard work was the cure for what ailed Henry. His newly built trading fort in Arguim Bay needed his attention, as did the ever-growing Vila do Infante. Every year new ships set out from Lagos to explore the Guinea coast. By 1446, over fifty caravels had reached Guinea; by 1448 over nine hundred slaves

*Statue of Henry the Navigator at Lagos, Portugal*

had been brought back to Portugal. Henry's claim to new territories was so great that, in 1454, the Pope gave him control of lands as far away as India.

That same year, Henry first sent out Alvise Cadamosto, who was to prove one of his most famous captains. Cadamosto was a 22-year-old Venetian seaman who landed in Sagres by accident. He was so impressed by all Prince Henry had accomplished, he promptly offered up his services. Over the next four years, Cadamosto's expeditions to Guinea would make him one of the most famous explorers and traders of the fifteenth century.

*Map of the West African coast, by Portuguese mapmaker Lazaro Luis*

Cadamosto first sailed to Santo Porto, Santa Maria, and Madeira, Henry's earliest island colonies in the Atlantic. Marveling at their prosperity (the rabbits were still on Santo Porto, but crops and cattle were thriving, too), he next sailed to the Canary Islands. These islands, whose ownership had long been disputed by Portugal and Castile, were nowhere near as civilized as Madeira. No doubt Prince Henry could have done a much better job, if the Canaries were under his command.

Sailing farther down the African coast, Cadamosto made a stop at Henry's booming trading post on Arguim Bay. By now, raiding had given way to trading in Henry's Africa. Caravans brought a steady stream of slaves and gold to Arguim, in exchange for the linens, woolen cloth, silver, grain, and salt offered by the Portuguese. As a trader, Cadamosto was most impressed by this profitable colonial outpost.

At Cape Blanco, Cadamosto interrupted his sea voyage for a short journey inland by camel. He took careful notes of all his conversations with Arab nomads and Tuareg tribesmen from the interior. Always a shrewd merchant, Cadamosto knew that more sales were made by diplomacy than by a show of force. He was determined to win the Africans' confidence and secure good trading relations for the future.

From Cape Blanco, Cadamosto sailed to Cape Verde, where he took another short trip inland on the Senegal River. Then it was down the coast another 50 miles (80 kilometers) to the country of a chief called Budomel.

Cadamosto spent a month as a guest at Budomel's village. He was the first European to stay so long in sub-Saharan Africa, and he returned with many amaz-

*Santo Antao, an island in the Cape Verde Islands group*

foot on the Cape Verde Islands; certainly he was the first to see a hippopotamus and to bring back elephant meat for Prince Henry to taste. Eventually Cadamosto reached the Geba River near today's city of Bissau. He was now so far south, his interpreters (Henry insisted that all his ships carry trained African interpreters) could no longer communicate with the region's inhabitants. Cadamosto has another "first" to his credit. As he finally and regretfully turned his ship northward for the return trip to Portugal, he saw four stars lying low on the horizon. By noting that fact in his log, Alvise Cadamosto became the first European ever to record seeing the most familiar constellation of the southern hemisphere, the Southern Cross.

# Chapter 9
# The Last Crusade

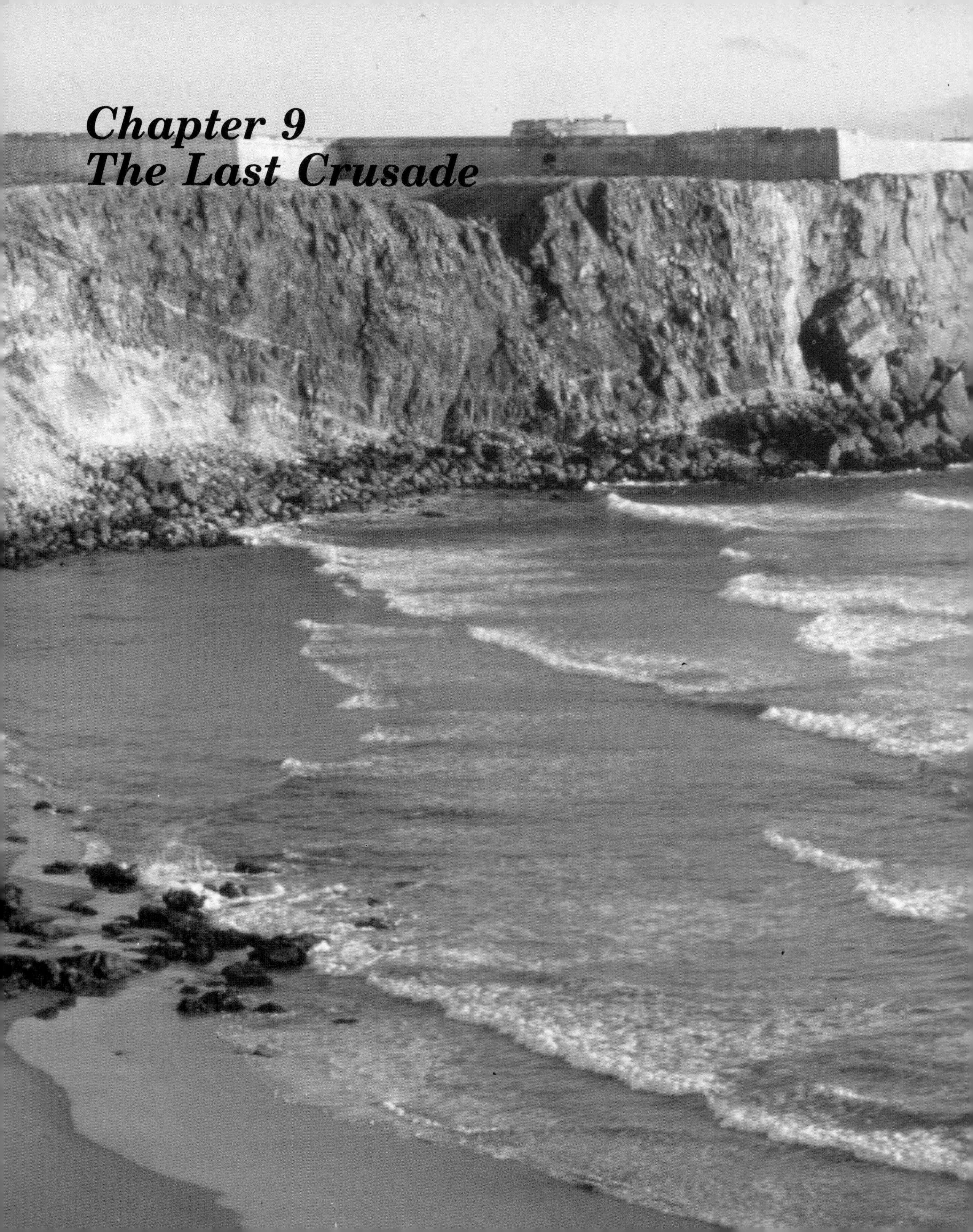

In 1458, Prince Henry's life was busy and full. His island colonies in the Atlantic were thriving. Mariners from all over Europe were flocking to Lagos in hopes of piloting his swift sailing caravels. At Sagres, Henry's cartographers were steadily recording the results of his African expeditions. With every map and chart, they pushed back the boundaries of the known world. His astronomers and instrument makers were constantly finding ways to improve the navigational tools that Henry's sailors depended on.

From Lisbon, King Afonso had long since made peace with Prince Henry. Recognizing how much Portugal stood to gain from his uncle's explorations, he wholeheartedly supported Henry's voyages. Perhaps best of all, at least one of Henry's captains was finally fulfilling his prince's dream of bringing salvation to the lost heathen souls of Africa.

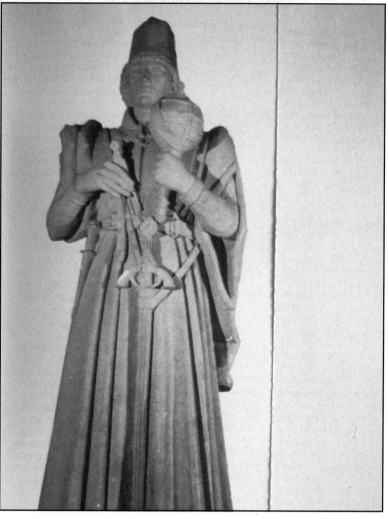

*Statue of Diogo Gomes*

Diogo Gomes was a faithful servant of Prince Henry's household and one of Henry's most trusted seamen. On his voyage of 1457, he had traveled all the way to the Geba River—the farthest point so far discovered—where he had found currents "so strong that no anchor could hold."

More importantly, on his return journey Gomes had finally broken the barrier of hostility that had kept the Portuguese from exploring the Gambia River. Where Nuno Tristão and Alvise Cadamosto had met with showers of poisoned arrows, Gomes managed to convince the Africans of his peaceful intentions. After

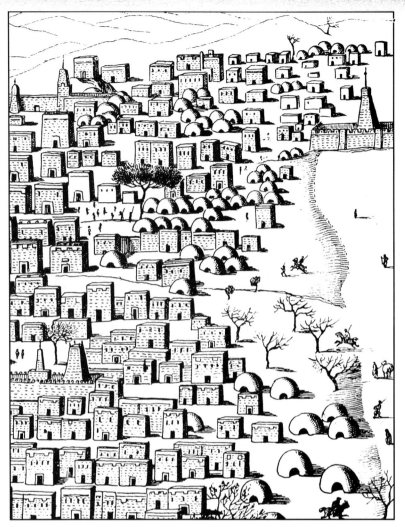

*The African city of Timbuktu, from an early engraving*

spending three days with Gomes, the very chief who had killed Tristão apologized for his actions and asked to be baptized a Christian. Wherever he went, Gomes seemed to meet with the same success.

Before he returned to Portugal, he had traveled nearly 500 miles (800 kilometers) up the Gambia into Africa's interior. He had met with merchants from the fabled Timbuktu and seen for himself the vast riches of the overland gold trade. He had converted whole villages to Christianity and won promises of goodwill from chiefs for miles around. Truly, Diogo Gomes was a captain after his prince's own heart.

Religion was never far from Prince Henry's mind these days. In 1453, the great Christian capital of Constantinople had finally fallen to the Muslim Turks. Later named Istanbul, this city in present-day Turkey had been the capital of the Eastern Roman Empire for almost 1,100 years. Though Pope Calixtus III called for a mighty European crusade to avenge this loss, only Portugal responded. Remembering his holy victory at Ceuta—and his tragic defeat at Tangier—Prince Henry was one of the first to heed the Christian call to arms.

But even Henry realized that Portugal alone could never hope to defeat the Turks at Constantinople. Instead, he and his nephew, King Afonso, decided to launch an attack on the Muslim city of Alcácer Ceguer. Situated between Ceuta and Tangier on the North African coast, Alcácer Ceguer promised to be an important port for Portugal.

Accordingly, King Afonso began his preparations. From Lagos he launched over two hundred ships, carrying some 25,000 soldiers. In charge of the entire expedition was the sixty-four-year-old Prince Henry. This time, Henry was determined to do it right. He personally supervised the positioning and firing of the heavy cannons. In less than a day, the aging crusader saw Alcácer Ceguer surrender unconditionally.

King Afonso left the terms of the peace treaty in his uncle's able hands. Though Prince Henry must have been tempted to punish the Moors for their own harsh terms at Tangier, he proved to be a fair and honorable negotiator. Asking only that all Christian prisoners be released unharmed, he allowed the Moors to leave the city peaceably with their wives, their children, and their personal property. "For," he ex-

*Victorious Turks entering Constantinople*

plained, "it was not to take their goods or force a ransom from them that the King of Portugal had come against them, but for the service of God."

Prince Henry returned home to Sagres. He had fought his last crusade, once again winning a victory for his country and his faith. His colonies in the Atlantic were flourishing, peaceful trade with Guinea was thriving, and Diogo Gomes was making Christian converts wherever he went.

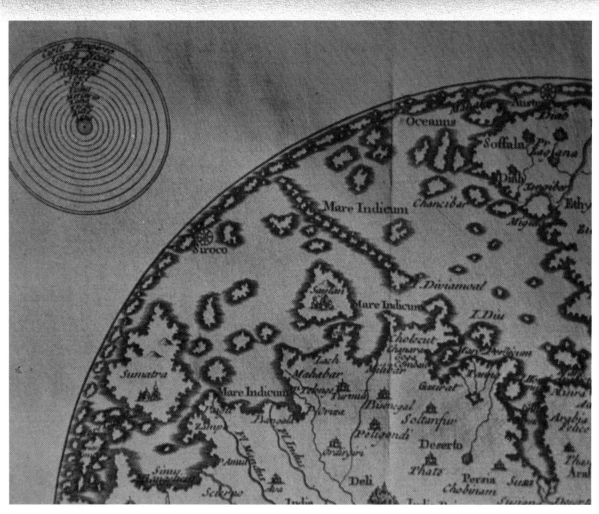

*Close-up of a corner of Fra Mauro's map of the world*

There was just one last task remaining. For three years, the great Venetian cartographer, Fra Mauro, had been working on a grand-scale map of the world. There would be no grinning sea monsters on this map, and no benevolent Christ smiling beatifically over his domain. Fra Mauro's map, which was based primarily on the information gathered by Prince Henry and his navigators, would show the world as it really was. Bays and promontories and islands; rivers and inlets; place names and proportions—all would be accurately, precisely, and mathematically drawn.

Fra Mauro's map was completed in 1459. In many ways, it represented the crowning achievement of

*Prince Henry*

Prince Henry's life. Science had replaced superstition, and knowledge had replaced invention. Finally Prince Henry of Portugal could rest. He was sixty-six years old, and his life had been strenuous by any standards. Diogo Gomes was with him during his final illness. Sorrowfully, this faithful captain wrote of his prince: "In the year of Christ 1460, the Lord Prince Henry fell sick in his own town . . . and of that sickness he died on Thursday, November 13, in the selfsame year. And King Afonso . . . made great mourning on the death of a Prince so mighty, who had sent out so many fleets, and had won so much from the land of Guinea, and had fought so constantly against the Infidels for the Faith."

Prince Henry of Portugal lived a life of great achievement—and great contradictions. He was born and bred as a devoutly Christian medieval knight. And yet, in his foresight and curiosity about the world, he proved himself a true Renaissance man. As a member of the Holy Order of Christ, he lived a chaste life of fasting and prayer. As a man of science, he scorned the Bible-based maps of the medieval world in favor of modern, geographically precise charts.

Prince Henry gloried in defeating the Infidel in holy battle. Yet his court at Sagres was filled with scholars of all races and religions. His quest for knowledge knew no religious or national boundaries. Muslims and Jews, Christians and pagans—all were welcome at Sagres if they could further the course of human understanding.

There were other contradictions. Throughout his lifetime, Henry was obsessed with ocean travel and exploration. He was called the Navigator because of his efforts to make navigation an exact science, rather than a matter of guesswork and luck. Yet he himself sailed on only three voyages, and he never had command of a ship. Prince Henry never did find the fabled Christian kingdom of Prester John. Long after Henry's death, however, Portuguese missionaries in Ethiopia would spread the gospel to thousands of Africans who may have been descended from that legendary king.

Prince Henry had little or no interest in personal gain. In fact, he died heavily in debt. But it was because of his voyages of exploration that tiny Portugal became one of the richest nations in Europe in the sixteenth and seventeenth centuries. Seamen inspired by Henry eventually went on to discover all-water routes to India and the East Indies. Portugal's colonial empire in the Far East was to dominate European trade for over 150 years.

Perhaps Prince Henry's greatest achievement was his navigation "school" at Sagres. The scholars of all races and religions, who gathered here to exchange ideas and solve problems, revolutionized the world. With Henry's encouragement, they turned navigation into a science, perfected the art of ship design, and drew the most accurate maps the world had ever known. Henry also introduced the practices of keeping precise sailing records and of sending interpreters on all voyages of exploration.

*Bas relief sculpture on Henry's fortress at Sagres*

*Portuguese navigator Bartolomeu Dias on his voyage toward the Cape of Good Hope*

With Henry's backing, his captains discovered more of the world than had ever been explored by Europeans. Inspired by their prince, these sailors learned to adapt to a wholly unfamiliar element—the ocean. Mile by mile they crept down the African coast, leaving stone columns to mark their progress. As long as the oceans of the world were thought to be unnavigable, they were barriers to human movement. Henry helped turn these barriers into highways—he helped the world become *known*. Throughout his life, Prince Henry strove to live up to the motto he had chosen in his youth: *"Talent de bien faire"*—the desire to do well. It is a testimony to Henry's invincible spirit that his vision did not die when he did.

In 1488, a Portuguese caravel captained by Bartolomeu Dias rounded the Cape of Good Hope at the southern tip of Africa. In 1498, another Portuguese captain named Vasco da Gama commanded four caravels past the Cape of Good Hope, across the Indian Ocean, and into the harbor of Calcutta in India. And in 1492, an Italian seaman named Christopher Columbus, who had married a Portuguese girl named Perestrello and spent hours studying his father-in-law's logbooks on the rabbity island of Santo Porto— sailed three caravels westward across the Atlantic in search of the East Indies. A new chapter in world history was about to begin. Prince Henry of Portugal wrote the introduction.

*Vasco da Gama meeting with the Lamorin of Calcutta to open up trade with India*

# *Appendix*

Map of Europe, Africa, and the Near East, a page from
Berlinghieri's fifteenth-century atlas

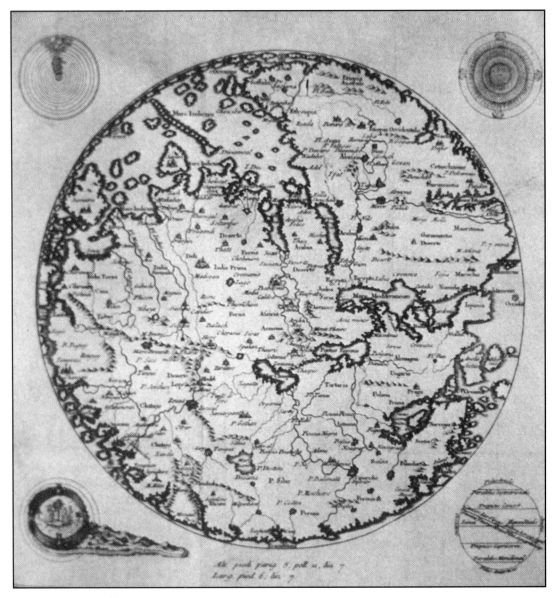

Fra Mauro's map of the world

# —*Some Models of Portuguese Ships*—

The nau S. Gabriel

Caravela redonda

Barca pescareza

Close-up of Henry leading other great navigators
on Lisbon's Monument to Discoveries

# Timeline of Events in Henry's Lifetime

**1394**—Prince Henry the Navigator is born

**1411**—Portugal begins massive preparations for the invasion of Ceuta in North Africa

**1415**—Henry's mother, Queen Philippa, dies; King John, Henry, and Portuguese troops storm and conquer Ceuta; Henry is made governor of Ceuta

**1418**—Henry takes up residence at Sagres on Cape St. Vincent

**1419**—Henry is made governor of the Algarve region of Portugal

**1420**—Henry's captains Teixeira and Zarco reach Santo Porto, one of the Madeira Islands; Henry is made grand master of the Order of Christ

**1421**—Zarco founds Funchal, the capital of the Madeiras

**1428**—Prince Pedro, Henry's brother, returns from his European travels, bringing Henry an Arab map and a copy of the *Book of Marco Polo*

**1432**—Goncalo Velho Cabral discovers the Azores Islands

**1433**—King John, Henry's father, dies and Duarte becomes king of Portugal

**1434**—Gil Eannes, one of Henry's captains, rounds West Africa's Cape Bojador

**1437**—Prince Henry and his troops are defeated in their invasion of Tangier; Portugal is required to return Ceuta to the Moors; Prince Fernando is held prisoner

**1438**—Overcome by grief and political troubles, King Duarte dies; a three-year quarrel begins about who will be his son Afonso's regent

**1441**—Duarte's widow, Queen Leonor, exiles herself to Spain; their son, young King Afonso, is left in the care of Prince Pedro; Nuno Tristão reaches Cape Blanco on the West African coast

**1442**—Prince John dies after a long illness

**1443**—Prince Fernando dies in prison in Tangier

**1444**—The town of Lagos, Portugal, holds its first slave auction

**1445**—Diníz Dias reaches the mouth of the Senegal River at Cape Verde

**1446**—Nuno Tristão reaches the mouth of the Gambia River, just north of the equator; sailing up the river, his crew is attacked and most of them are killed

**1448**—Henry builds a fort on Africa's west coast at Arguim Bay

**1449**—Prince Pedro is killed in battle

**1453**—Constantinople falls to the Turks

**1454**—The Pope gives Henry control of lands as far away as India

**1456**—Alvise Cadamosto reaches the Cape Verde Islands

**1457**—Diogo Gomes travels up the Gambia River and makes many converts to Christianity

**1459**—Venetian cartographer Fra Mauro completes his map of the world, based largely on information from Henry's navigators

**1460**—Henry dies in Sagres on November 13

## Glossary of Terms

**adamant**—Rigidly insistent

**ambergris**—A waxy material used in perfumes

**astrolabe**—An instrument used by sailors to determine the positions of stars and planets

**attar of roses**—A fragrant oil extracted from rose petals

**barter**—To exchange goods without using money

**becalmed**—Not able to sail because of no wind

**blasphemous**—Irreverent

**bluff**—A steep cliff or bank

**caravan**—A long string of pack animals

**chaste**—Pure

**chivalry**—The courtesy and high principles of a knight

**christened**—Baptized; named; given a name at the time of baptism

**citadel**—Fortress

**councillors**—Advisors

**damask**—A patterned fabric originally woven in Damascus

**defiance**—The act of challenging or resisting

**gale**—A fierce storm

**garrison**—A military post

**heathen**—Someone considered to have no faith or a false faith

**heresy**—A religious belief considered to be outrageous or false

**hostage**—Someone held as a prisoner to be exchanged for something

**infidel**—Unbeliever

**jinxed**—Doomed to bad luck or failure

**jousting**—A horseback tournament in which opponents with long spears charge at each other and try to knock each other off the horse

**knot**—Another name for a nautical mile, which is slightly longer than a land mile

**languish**—To be depressed, weakened, or neglected

**lateen sails**—Triangular sails

**marauding**—Roaming around looking for opportunities to raid or invade

**medieval**—Occurring in the Middle Ages, roughly A.D. 500 to A.D. 1500

**mercenary**—A soldier who fights only for money, rather than out of loyalty

**mosque**—A Muslim house of prayer and worship

**musk**—A substance from the musk deer used in making perfumes

**pension**—A regular payment to a person who is retired

**plague**—A widespread deadly disease

**promontory**—A point of land sticking out into a body of water

**ransom**—Money paid for the release of a hostage or prisoner

**regent**—The guardian of a child king or queen, who rules until the child is old enough to take the throne

**rout**—A complete defeat

**skirmish**—A minor fight

**squire**—Someone who serves a knight

**stoically**—Holding back a feeling or response

**strait**—A narrow channel of water between two larger bodies of water

**sub-Saharan Africa**—Africa south of the Sahara Desert

**surrogate**—Someone who acts in place of another

**travelogue**—A travel guide to a certain area

**treasure trove**—A valuable discovery

# Bibliography

**For further reading, see:**

Bradford, Ernle D. *A Wind from the North: the Life of Henry the Navigator*. NY: Harcourt, Brace. 1960.

Buehr, Walter. *The Portuguese Explorers*. NY: Putnam. 1966.

Chubb, Thomas Caldecot. *Prince Henry the Navigator and the Highways of the Sea*. NY: Viking Press. 1970.

Fisher, Leonard Everett. *Prince Henry the Navigator*. NY: Macmillan. 1990.

Jacobs, William Jay. *Prince Henry, the Navigator*. NY: Franklin Watts. 1973.

Sanceau, Elaine. *Henry the Navigator: the Story of a Great Prince and His Times*. NY: W. W. Norton & Co. 1947.

Ure, John. *Prince Henry the Navigator*. NY: Constable. 1977.

# Index

**Page numbers in boldface type indicate illustrations.**

# Picture Identifications for Chapter Opening Spreads

6-7—View of Ceuta

12-13—Old Lisbon

24-25—The Rock of Gibraltar

40-41—Vineyard in the village of Seixal, with Portugal's rugged north coast in the background

52-53—A fortress on the coast at Tangier, Morocco

61-62—Present-day view of Timbuktu

72-73—Black lava sand on tha beach of Sao Felipe, Fogo, Cape Verde Islands, West Africa

86-87—The southeast ccast of La Gomera, Canary Islands

98-99—Sagres, location of Henry's fortress and navigation school

## Picture Acknowledgments

Biblioteca Nacional, Portugal—27, 49, 58, 89, 93

Museu de Marinha, Lisbon—63, 64 (margin), 65 (2 pictures), 112 (3 pictures)

Courtesy Museum of the American Numismatic Association—4

North Wind Picture Archives—9, 22, 34 (bottom), 47 (margin), 75, 76, 77, 79, 84, 91, 96

Odyssey Productions: © Robert Frerck—5, 52-53, 85, 86-87, 92, 98-99, 107, 113

Photri—23, 24-25, 56, 60-61, 95

Portuguese Tourist Bureau, New York—12-13, 31

H. Armstrong Roberts: © George Hunter—40-41, 47 (top)

Sociedade Historica da Independencia de Portugal—2, 14 (2 pictures), 15, 21, 59, 100, 104, 111

Stock Montage, Inc.—6-7, 11, 18, 29, 34 (margin), 36, 37, 38, 39, 45, 62, 64 (bottom), 67, 70, 71, 90, 101, 103, 105, 108, 109

SuperStock, Inc.—46, 72-73, 82, 97

UPI/Bettmann—110

Valan Photos: © V. Wilkinson—50; © Val & Alan Wilkinson—55

## About the Author

Charnan Simon grew up in Ohio, Georgia, Oregon, and Washington State. She holds a B.A. degree in English Literature from Carleton College in Northfield, Minnesota, and an M.A. in English Literature from the University of Chicago. She worked for children's trade book companies after college and became the managing editor of *Cricket* magazine before beginning her career as a free-lance writer. Ms. Simon has written dozens of books and articles for young people and especially likes writing—and reading—history, biography, and fiction of all sorts. She lives in Chicago with her husband and two daughters.